Edition

Travel to Pittsburgh Pennsylvania

2023
People Who Know
Publishing
Jack Ross

Forward: In this book, People Who Know Publishing will provide a travel guide of 101+ things to see, do and visit in Pittsburgh Pennsylvania. We strive to make our guides as comprehensive and complete as possible. We publish travel guides on cities and countries all over the world. Feel free to check out our complete list of travel guides here:

People Who Know Publishing partners with local experts to produce travel guides on various locations. We differentiate ourselves from other travel books by focusing on areas not typically covered by others. Our guides include a detailed history of the location and its population. In addition to covering all of the "must see" areas of a location such as museums and local sights, we also provide up-to-date restaurant suggestions and local food traditions.

To make a request for a travel guide on a particular area or to join our email list to stay updated on travel tips from local experts sign up here: https://mailchi.mp/c74b62620b1f/travel-books

Be sure to confirm restaurants, addresses, and phone numbers as those may have changed since the book was published.

About the Author:

Jack Ross is a college student who was born in Westchester County, NY. He's an expert on the local "in the know" tips of the area and is an authority on Westchester and its towns. He's been featured in several publications including Business Insider and CNBC for his books.

During his spare time, he writes, plays tennis and golf and enjoys all water sports (including his latest favorite, the eFoil). Jack also enjoys traveling and is a food connoisseur throughout Westchester. Jack travels consistently and has been to majority of the states in the U.S.

Sign up for our email list to get inside access to the towns and places we cover!
>> https://mailchi.mp/c74b62620b1f/travel-books
>> https://mailchi.mp/c74b62620b1f/travel-books

Table of Contents

VII

Pittsburgh Pennsylvania

State: Pennsylvania

Population: 302,971

Ranking in U.S.: N/A

County: Allegheny County

Founded: 1758

Tag line: N/A

Introduction

"Pittsburgh is my heart. When I die, I'm going to leave my heart in Pittsburgh." - Joe Manganiello

Pittsburgh, often referred to as the "Steel City" or the "City of Bridges," is a vibrant and historic metropolis located in the western part of Pennsylvania, USA. Nestled at the confluence of the Allegheny, Monongahela, and Ohio Rivers, this city has a rich industrial heritage, a thriving cultural scene, and a unique blend of old-world charm and modern innovation.

Founded in 1758, Pittsburgh's early growth was fueled by the steel industry, earning it a reputation as an industrial powerhouse in the late 19th and early 20th centuries. However, the city has since transformed itself into a hub for technology, education, healthcare, and the arts.

Pittsburgh's skyline is defined by its iconic bridges, including the bright yellow Roberto Clemente Bridge and the elegant Smithfield Street Bridge, which add character and connectivity to the city. The cityscape is a mesmerizing mix of historic architecture, modern skyscrapers, and lush green spaces.

Known for its world-class universities and research institutions, including Carnegie Mellon University and the University of Pittsburgh, Pittsburgh has become a center for innovation and technology, particularly in fields like robotics, artificial intelligence, and healthcare. This transformation has earned it the nickname "Roboburgh."

Sports are a significant part of the city's culture, with passionate fans supporting the Pittsburgh Steelers (NFL), Pittsburgh Penguins (NHL), and Pittsburgh Pirates (MLB). The city's sports history is celebrated in venues like the Heinz History Center.

Pittsburgh's diverse neighborhoods offer a variety of experiences, from the cultural hotspots of the Strip District to the trendy restaurants and shops in Lawrenceville. The city's food scene is a testament to its melting pot of cultures, with offerings ranging from traditional Pittsburgh pierogies to international cuisine.

Cultural institutions like the Carnegie Museums, the Andy Warhol Museum, and the Pittsburgh Symphony Orchestra provide enriching experiences for residents and visitors alike. Additionally, Pittsburgh hosts numerous festivals and events throughout the year, celebrating its heritage and creativity.

Travel to Pittsburgh Pennsylvania

In recent years, Pittsburgh has gained recognition for its commitment to sustainability and green initiatives, further enhancing its reputation as a forward-thinking city.

Whether you're exploring its history, enjoying its cultural offerings, or marveling at its scenic riverfronts, Pittsburgh invites you to experience a city that seamlessly blends its industrial past with its innovative future.

History

French and British Colonial Periods:
In the mid-18th century, the area that would become Pittsburgh was hotly contested by European powers. The French built Fort Duquesne at the confluence of the Allegheny and Monongahela Rivers in 1754. In 1758, during the French and Indian War, British forces captured and renamed it Fort Pitt in honor of British Prime Minister William Pitt the Elder.

Early American Settlement:
After the American Revolution, the region saw an influx of settlers, including many Scotch-Irish and German immigrants. Pittsburgh's strategic location at the intersection of three rivers made it a vital transportation and trade hub.

Early Indigenous Inhabitants:
Before European settlement, the Pittsburgh region was home to several Native American tribes, including the Delaware, Shawnee, and Seneca. These indigenous peoples relied on the rivers and abundant natural resources for their livelihoods.

Travel to Pittsburgh Pennsylvania

Labor and Union Movements:
The rapid growth of industry led to labor disputes and the rise of labor unions. The Homestead Strike of 1892, involving workers at Andrew Carnegie's Homestead Steel Works, was one of the most significant labor conflicts in U.S. history.

The City of Bridges:
Pittsburgh's topography, with its rivers and steep hillsides, necessitated the construction of numerous bridges. The city is known for having more bridges (over 440) than any other in the world, including the iconic yellow Three Sisters Bridges and the Roberto Clemente Bridge.

Post-Industrial Decline:
In the mid-20th century, the steel industry faced decline due to factors such as foreign competition and changes in manufacturing technology. This led to economic hardship and population loss in Pittsburgh and other industrial cities.

Industrialization and the Steel Industry:
Pittsburgh's transformation into an industrial powerhouse began in the early 19th century, driven by the coal and iron ore deposits in the surrounding hills. The city's steel industry, led by companies like U.S. Steel and Carnegie Steel (founded by Andrew Carnegie), dominated the global market. Pittsburgh earned its nickname, the "Steel City," during this era.

Travel to Pittsburgh Pennsylvania

Renaissance and Transformation:
In the 1950s and '60s, Pittsburgh underwent a renaissance period, investing in urban renewal, infrastructure, and education. This transformation laid the groundwork for the city's shift toward a diversified economy, focusing on healthcare, technology, education, and finance.

Education and Innovation Hub:
Pittsburgh is home to several world-renowned universities and research institutions, including Carnegie Mellon University and the University of Pittsburgh. These institutions have played a pivotal role in driving innovation, particularly in fields like robotics, artificial intelligence, and healthcare.

Modern Pittsburgh:
Today, Pittsburgh is a thriving, dynamic city with a diversified economy, a vibrant arts and culture scene, and a strong focus on sustainability. It has shed its image as a steel town and embraced its identity as a hub for technology, education, and healthcare.

Economy

One of Pittsburgh's largest and fastest-growing sectors is healthcare and life sciences. The city is home to world-class medical institutions like the University of Pittsburgh Medical Center (UPMC) and Allegheny Health Network, which drive innovation, research, and patient care.
Biotechnology and pharmaceutical companies also have a strong presence in the region.

Pittsburgh has emerged as a leader in technology and innovation, particularly in fields like robotics, artificial intelligence (AI), and autonomous vehicles.
Carnegie Mellon University is a major contributor to these advancements.
Tech companies, research labs, and startups have thrived, attracting talent and investment to the region.
The establishment of tech incubators and co-working spaces has further nurtured the local tech ecosystem.

The city's universities and research institutions, including Carnegie Mellon University and the University of Pittsburgh, play a crucial role in driving research, development, and intellectual capital.
Pittsburgh's strong educational base also supports a skilled workforce that contributes to various industries.

Pittsburgh has a growing financial and business services sector. The city hosts numerous banks, investment firms, and insurance companies.
The presence of major financial institutions contributes to the city's economic stability.

While the steel industry has declined, Pittsburgh remains connected to the energy sector. The region has seen growth in renewable energy, natural gas, and clean technology industries.
The proximity to shale gas reserves in the Marcellus and Utica Shales has attracted energy-related investment.

Although steel production has decreased significantly, manufacturing still plays a role in Pittsburgh's economy. The region is involved in advanced manufacturing, including aerospace, machinery, and electronics.

Transportation Systems

Roadways: Pittsburgh has an extensive network of roads and highways, making it easily accessible by car. Major routes include Interstate 376, Interstate 279, and several state routes. The city's unique topography, with hills and rivers, can make driving challenging in some areas.

Bridges: Pittsburgh is known for its numerous bridges, which connect different neighborhoods across its rivers. These bridges are essential for commuting within the city.

Public Transit: The Port Authority of Allegheny County operates the public transit system, including buses and light rail. The "T" (short for Trolley) is a light rail system that serves various neighborhoods, including downtown Pittsburgh.

Bicycling: Pittsburgh has made efforts to become more bike-friendly, with dedicated bike lanes, trails, and bike-sharing programs. The city's terrain can be hilly, but there are options for both recreational and commuter cyclists.

Air Travel: Pittsburgh International Airport is the primary airport serving the region. It offers domestic and international flights and is located about 20 miles west of downtown Pittsburgh.

Rail: While passenger rail services are limited, Amtrak operates the Capitol Limited and Pennsylvanian routes, providing connections to other cities like Washington, D.C., Philadelphia, and Chicago.

Inclines: Pittsburgh's historic inclines, such as the Duquesne Incline and Monongahela Incline, are unique forms of transportation that take passengers up steep hillsides while offering stunning views of the city.

Waterways: Pittsburgh's location at the junction of three rivers has historically made water transportation significant. While not a primary mode of transportation today, the rivers still see some commercial traffic, including river cruises and recreational boating.

Neighborhoods

Downtown: Pittsburgh's central business district is home to iconic skyscrapers, cultural institutions, and restaurants. It's a bustling hub for both work and entertainment.

Strip District: A historic market district with a vibrant food scene, specialty shops, and a mix of residential and commercial spaces.

Lawrenceville: A trendy neighborhood known for its art scene, boutiques, and restaurants. It's popular among young professionals and artists.

South Side: This neighborhood along the Monongahela River offers a lively nightlife with bars, clubs, and a mix of housing options.

Squirrel Hill: A diverse and culturally rich neighborhood with a strong sense of community. It's known for its tree-lined streets, shops, and restaurants.

Shadyside: An upscale neighborhood with historic homes, high-end boutiques, and a thriving dining scene.

Oakland: Home to several universities and cultural institutions, including the University of Pittsburgh and Carnegie Museums.

East Liberty: Undergoing redevelopment, this neighborhood features a mix of modern apartments, shops, and dining options.

Bloomfield: Known as Pittsburgh's "Little Italy," it has a vibrant restaurant scene and a strong Italian influence.

Food

Primanti Bros. Sandwich: Perhaps the most famous Pittsburgh dish, the Primanti Bros. sandwich features grilled meat, coleslaw, tomato slices, and French fries piled high between two thick slices of Italian bread.

Pierogies: Pittsburgh has a strong Eastern European influence, and pierogies (dumplings filled with ingredients like potato, cheese, or meat) are a beloved local comfort food. You can find them in many Pittsburgh restaurants and even at PNC Park during baseball games.

City Chicken: Despite the name, city chicken is actually a dish made with skewered and breaded chunks of pork or veal, resembling a chicken drumstick. It's typically served with gravy.

Haluski: Another Eastern European favorite, haluski is a dish made with pan-fried cabbage and egg noodles, often flavored with butter and onions.

Kielbasa: Pittsburgh's Polish heritage is evident in its love for kielbasa, a delicious sausage often served with sauerkraut or on a sandwich.

Fish Sandwich: Lenten Fridays in Pittsburgh often mean indulging in a fish sandwich, typically made with a large fried fish fillet, lettuce, tomato, and tartar sauce on a bun. Many local churches and eateries offer their own version during this time.

Chipped Ham Sandwich: Chipped ham is thinly sliced and served on a sandwich, often with mustard or barbecue sauce. It's a simple but beloved local favorite.

Banana Split: The banana split, a classic American dessert, has a special connection to Pittsburgh. It was reportedly invented in the city in the early 20th century by a pharmacy soda jerk.

Here are our ten favorite restaurant recommendations!

1.Cure: A renowned restaurant in Lawrenceville, Cure focuses on farm-to-table cuisine and features a frequently changing menu that showcases seasonal ingredients. It's known for its creative dishes and charcuterie.

2.Morcilla: Another gem in Lawrenceville, Morcilla offers Spanish-inspired cuisine with a focus on small plates, including a wide variety of tapas and an extensive selection of house-made sausages.

3.Dinette: Located in East Liberty, Dinette is known for its artisanal pizzas and farm-to-table approach to dining. Their wood-fired pizzas and seasonal salads are particularly popular.

4.Gaucho Parrilla Argentina: This Strip District restaurant is famous for its wood-fired Argentinean-style meats and empanadas. It offers a casual, yet flavorful dining experience.

5.Altius: Situated on Mount Washington, Altius provides stunning views of the Pittsburgh skyline along with a sophisticated dining experience. It's known for its modern American cuisine and exceptional service.

6.Butcher and the Rye: Located downtown, this restaurant offers a diverse selection of whiskey and a menu that combines rustic and refined dishes, including creative charcuterie and artisanal cocktails.

7.*Casbah: A Mediterranean-inspired restaurant in Shadyside, Casbah offers a cozy atmosphere and a menu featuring dishes influenced by the flavors of North Africa, Southern Europe, and the Middle East.*

8.*Apteka: A unique vegan and Eastern European-inspired restaurant in Bloomfield, Apteka is known for its inventive pierogies, vegan kielbasa, and creative cocktails.*

9.*Leo. a public house: A gastropub located in the North Side, Leo offers a menu with an emphasis on locally sourced ingredients and craft beers, making it a favorite among food and beer enthusiasts.*

10.*Spoon: This East Liberty restaurant specializes in contemporary American cuisine with a focus on fresh and seasonal ingredients. It's known for its elegant and well-crafted dishes.*

Nightlife

South Side: Pittsburgh's South Side is known for its energetic nightlife. It's packed with bars, clubs, and restaurants that cater to a diverse crowd. Carson Street is the main thoroughfare for nightlife activities, offering numerous options for drinks and entertainment.

Lawrenceville: Lawrenceville has emerged as a trendy nightlife destination, with a variety of bars, breweries, and music venues. You can find everything from craft cocktails to live indie music performances.

Cultural District: Downtown Pittsburgh's Cultural District is home to theaters, art galleries, and entertainment venues. After catching a show, you can explore the district's bars and lounges for a post-performance drink.

North Shore: This area, near Heinz Field and PNC Park, is a popular spot on game nights, with sports bars and restaurants that offer a lively atmosphere. You can enjoy drinks and views of the city's iconic bridges along the riverfront.

Strip District: The Strip District comes alive during the daytime as a bustling market, but it also has several bars and clubs that keep the party going into the night. It's a great place for late-night dining options too.

Shadyside: Shadyside offers a more upscale nightlife experience with wine bars, cocktail lounges, and upscale restaurants. It's a great choice for a sophisticated night out.

Local Traditions & Customs

Yinz: "Yinz" is a distinctive Pittsburgh dialect term, similar to "y'all" in the South or "you guys" in other regions. It's used as a colloquial way to address a group of people. For example, "Are yinz going to the game?"

Black and Gold: Pittsburghers are known for their fervent support of the city's sports teams, particularly the Pittsburgh Steelers (NFL), Pittsburgh Penguins (NHL), and Pittsburgh Pirates (MLB). The colors black and gold are worn proudly by fans, and game days are often a big part of local culture.

Pittsburghese: The city has its own unique way of speaking, with distinct pronunciations and vocabulary. Some common Pittsburghese words include "gum bands" for rubber bands, "jagoff" for an annoying person, and "redd up" for clean up.

Pierogi Fridays: During Lent, many Pittsburghers participate in the tradition of eating pierogies on Fridays, often at church fish fries or local restaurants. This custom reflects the city's strong Eastern European influence.

Fishing on Good Friday: On Good Friday, it's a longstanding tradition for some Pittsburghers to go fishing. It's believed to bring good luck, and it's also a practical way to enjoy the spring weather.

Pittsburgh Parking Chairs: In the winter, when residents shovel out their parking spaces on the street, it's common to use a chair or other item to reserve that space. This practice is widely accepted, and moving someone else's parking chair can lead to disputes.

What to buy?

Terrible Towel: The Terrible Towel is an iconic symbol of Pittsburgh Steelers fandom. You can find them in various colors and designs at sports stores, souvenir shops, and even during Steelers games.

Pittsburgh Sports Gear: Whether you're a fan of the Steelers, Penguins, or Pirates, Pittsburgh has a wide range of sports apparel and memorabilia to choose from.

Pittsburgh Food Items: Bring a taste of Pittsburgh home with you by purchasing local food items like Primanti Bros. coleslaw and fry kits, Heinz ketchup products (the company is headquartered in Pittsburgh), or a selection of pierogies.

Iron City Beer: Iron City is a well-known Pittsburgh beer brand. Consider picking up some Iron City beer or merchandise as a memento of your visit.

Local Art and Crafts: Pittsburgh has a thriving arts scene, and you can find unique artwork, handmade crafts, and pottery at local galleries and markets such as the Pittsburgh Public Market.

City-Themed Merchandise: Look for Pittsburgh-themed merchandise like T-shirts, mugs, keychains, and magnets that feature the city's skyline, bridges, and other iconic landmarks.

Local Jewelry: Many Pittsburgh artisans create unique jewelry inspired by the city's skyline and bridges. Consider buying a piece of locally made jewelry as a keepsake.

Finally, here are the five most famous people from the city!

1.Local Jewelry: Many Pittsburgh artisans create unique jewelry inspired by the city's skyline and bridges. Consider buying a piece of locally made jewelry as a keepsake.Fred Rogers: Fred Rogers, beloved as "Mister Rogers," was a television icon and children's educator. He hosted the long-running children's show "Mister Rogers' Neighborhood," which had a profound impact on generations of children and continues to be cherished worldwide.

2.Andy Warhol: Andy Warhol, a leading figure in the pop art movement, was born in Pittsburgh. His iconic artwork, including the Campbell's Soup Cans and Marilyn Monroe portraits, remains influential in the world of contemporary art.

3.August Wilson: August Wilson, an acclaimed playwright, was born and raised in Pittsburgh. He is best known for his ten-play series, "The Pittsburgh Cycle," which explores African American life in the United States throughout the 20th century. Wilson's work has won numerous awards, including Pulitzer Prizes.

4.Andrew Carnegie: Andrew Carnegie, an industrialist and philanthropist, was one of the wealthiest individuals in the late 19th and early 20th centuries. He played a significant role in the development of the steel industry in Pittsburgh and is known for his extensive philanthropic efforts, including the funding of libraries and education.

5.Dan Marino: Dan Marino, a Pro Football Hall of Famer, is one of the most famous quarterbacks in NFL history. Though he was born in Pittsburgh, he achieved fame while playing for the Miami Dolphins, where he set numerous passing records during his career.

101+ things to do in the city

1. Visit the Andy Warhol Museum.
2. Explore the Carnegie Museum of Natural History.
3. Take a ride on the Duquesne Incline.
4. Stroll through Phipps Conservatory and Botanical Gardens.
5. Attend a Pittsburgh Pirates baseball game at PNC Park.
6. Explore the National Aviary.
7. Visit the Carnegie Science Center.
8. Take a walk along the Three Rivers Heritage Trail.
9. Tour the Mattress Factory, a contemporary art museum.
10. Experience the historic Strip District's food markets.
11. Explore the Pittsburgh Zoo & PPG Aquarium.
12. Take a cruise on the Gateway Clipper Fleet.
13. Discover the history of the Heinz History Center.
14. Visit Fallingwater, Frank Lloyd Wright's masterpiece
15. Attend a Pittsburgh Steelers football game at Heinz Field.
16. Explore the ToonSeum, a museum dedicated to comics and cartoons.
17. Enjoy a scenic drive through Schenley Park.
18. Take a walk along the North Shore Riverfront Park.
19. Visit the Soldiers & Sailors Memorial Hall and Museum.
20. Explore Randyland, a colorful art installation in the North Side.
21. Attend a concert at Stage AE.
22. Experience the historic Kennywood amusement park.
23. Visit the Pittsburgh Center for the Arts.
24. Explore the South Side Works, a shopping and entertainment district.
25. Attend a show at the Benedum Center for the Performing Arts.
26. Go kayaking or paddleboarding on the city's rivers.
27. Discover the Children's Museum of Pittsburgh.
28. Take a tour of Allegheny Cemetery.
29. Explore the historic Carrie Furnaces.
30. Attend a Pittsburgh Symphony Orchestra performance.
31. Visit the Clemente Museum, dedicated to baseball legend Roberto Clemente.
32. Enjoy a picnic in Frick Park.
33. Take a ride on the Monongahela Incline.
34. Explore Bicycle Heaven, the world's largest bicycle museum.
35. Visit the Western Pennsylvania Model Railroad Museum.
36. Explore the Roberto Clemente Bridge.
37. Attend a live theater performance at City Theatre.
38. Take a walk in Highland Park and see the Pittsburgh Reservoir.
39. Discover the August Wilson House, the childhood home of the playwright.
40. Enjoy a jazz performance at the Manchester Craftsmen's Guild.

41. Take a bike ride on the Great Allegheny Passage trail.
42. Attend a Pittsburgh Ballet Theatre performance.
43. Explore the Beechview-Seldom Seen Greenway.
44. Visit the Pittsburgh Glass Center.
45. Experience the beauty of Raccoon Creek State Park (near Pittsburgh).
46. Attend a Pittsburgh Opera performance.
47. Visit the Bicycle Museum of America.
48. Explore the Johnny Angel's Ginchy Stuff and Music Museum.
49. Attend a comedy show at the Arcade Comedy Theater.
50. Take a scenic drive through Ohiopyle State Park (near Pittsburgh).
51. Visit the Fort Pitt Museum.
52. Explore the historical reenactments at Bushy Run Battlefield.
53. Attend a performance at the New Hazlett Theater.
54. Take a scenic drive through Laurel Highlands (near Pittsburgh).
55. Visit the Bayernhof Museum, a unique historic mansion.
56. Explore the Frick Art & Historical Center.
57. Attend a live music performance at Club Cafe.
58. Visit the Maridon Museum, dedicated to Asian art and culture.
59. Explore the Westmoreland Museum of American Art
60. Attend a performance at the Pittsburgh Playhouse.
61. Take a self-guided architectural walking tour in Oakland.
62. Visit the West End Overlook for panoramic city views.
63. Explore the Pittsburgh Vintage Grand Prix.
64. Attend a show at the Arcade Comedy Theater.
65. Take a scenic drive through Forbes State Forest (near Pittsburgh).
66. Visit the Tull Family Theater, an independent cinema.
67. Explore the historic Hartwood Acres Park and Mansion.
68. Attend a performance by the Pittsburgh New Music Ensemble.
69. Take a scenic drive through Chestnut Ridge Park (near Pittsburgh).
70. Visit the Todd Nature Reserve in Sarver (near Pittsburgh).
71. Explore the Pittsburgh Cultural Trust Gallery Crawl.
72. Attend a performance by Attack Theatre.
73. Take a scenic drive through McConnell's Mill State Park (near Pittsburgh).
74. Visit the Southern Alleghenies Museum of Art (in Ligonier, near Pittsburgh).
75. Explore the Pittsburgh Glass Art Studio.
76. Attend a performance by Quantum Theatre.
77. Take a scenic drive through Beaver Creek State Park (near Pittsburgh).
78. Visit the Westmoreland Heritage Trail (near Pittsburgh).
79. Explore the Wood Street Galleries for contemporary art.
80. Attend a performance by Bricolage Production Company.
81. Take a scenic drive through Raccoon Creek State Park (near Pittsburgh).

82.Visit the Harmony Museum (in Harmony, near Pittsburgh).

83.Explore the Pittsburgh Playwrights Theatre Company.

84.Attend a performance by The Pillow Project.

85.Take a scenic drive through Linn Run State Park (near Pittsburgh).

86.Visit the Westmoreland County Historical

87.Explore the Andy Warhol Bridge.

88.Attend a performance by the Attack Theatre.

89.Take a scenic drive through Yellow Creek State Park (near Pittsburgh).

90.Visit the Allegheny Observatory.

91.Explore the Wood Street Commons for public art installations.

92.Attend a performance by the No Name Players.

93.Take a scenic drive through Keystone State Park (near Pittsburgh).

94.Visit the Soldiers & Sailors Memorial Hall Museum.

95.Explore the USS Requin, a historic submarine museum.

96.Attend a performance by the Jewish Theatre of Pittsburgh.

97.Take a scenic drive through Oil Creek State Park (near Pittsburgh).

98.Visit the Penn Brewery for traditional German beer and cuisine.

99.Explore the Soldiers & Sailors Memorial Hall & Museum.

100.Attend a performance by the Attack Theatre.

101.Take a scenic drive through Opossum Lake (near Pittsburgh).

102.Visit the August Wilson Center for African American Culture.

103.Explore the Wood Street T Station for its art installations.

104.Attend a performance by Pittsburgh Musical Theater.

105.Take a scenic drive through Lake Arthur (near Pittsburgh).

106.Visit the Andy Warhol Museum.

107.Explore the Nationality Rooms at the University of Pittsburgh.

108.Attend a performance by PICT Classic Theatre.

109.Take a scenic drive through Blue Knob State Park (near Pittsburgh).

110.Visit the Contemporary Craft gallery.

1.Visit the Andy Warhol Museum.

Visiting the Andy Warhol Museum in Pittsburgh is a captivating experience that takes you on a journey through the life and works of one of the most influential artists of the 20th century, Andy Warhol. The museum is the largest institution in North America dedicated to a single artist, making it a cultural gem that art enthusiasts and curious minds shouldn't miss.

As you step into the museum, you'll find yourself immersed in the world of Andy Warhol. The museum's extensive collection features a wide array of Warhol's creations, including his iconic pop art pieces, such as the famous Campbell's Soup Cans, Marilyn Monroe portraits, and Brillo Box sculptures. You'll have the opportunity to explore his groundbreaking contributions to the art world, which challenged traditional notions of art and celebrity.

The museum not only showcases Warhol's art but also provides insights into his life and the creative process. You can explore his personal artifacts, from his wigs and sunglasses to his cameras and paintbrushes. These intimate glimpses into Warhol's life offer a deeper understanding of the man behind the art.

The museum also features a screening room where you can watch some of Warhol's experimental films, which played a significant role in shaping modern cinema. These films reveal his innovative and avant-garde approach to the medium.

Additionally, the Andy Warhol Museum often hosts special exhibitions that highlight different aspects of his work and influence. These exhibitions provide fresh perspectives on his art and its ongoing impact on contemporary culture.

Overall, a visit to the Andy Warhol Museum is a unique and enriching experience that celebrates the life, art, and legacy of an artist who forever changed the way we perceive and create art. Whether you're a dedicated art aficionado or just looking for a fascinating cultural outing, the museum offers an inspiring journey into the world of Andy Warhol.

2.Explore the Carnegie Museum of Natural History.

Exploring the Carnegie Museum of Natural History in Pittsburgh is a captivating and educational experience that allows you to journey through the wonders of the natural world. This prestigious institution, part of the Carnegie Museums complex, is one of the leading natural history museums in the United States and offers a diverse range of exhibits and collections that cater to all ages and interests.

Upon entering the museum, you'll be greeted by a towering dinosaur skeleton, setting the tone for the many prehistoric wonders you're about to discover. Some highlights and key attractions to explore within the museum include:

Dinosaur Hall: Step back in time and marvel at the impressive collection of dinosaur fossils, including the renowned Diplodocus carnegii skeleton, which was one of the first fully assembled dinosaur skeletons in the world.

Mineral and Gem Collection: View a dazzling array of minerals and gems, including rare and precious stones that showcase the Earth's geological beauty.

Hall of North American Wildlife: Immerse yourself in the lifelike dioramas that depict North American animals in their natural habitats, providing a unique opportunity to observe and appreciate the region's biodiversity.

Ancient Egypt: Explore the museum's extensive collection of artifacts from ancient Egypt, including mummies, sarcophagi, and other fascinating relics that offer a glimpse into this ancient civilization's history.

Hall of Botany: Journey into the world of plants and botany with a focus on native and exotic plant species. The exhibit provides insight into plant diversity, growth, and adaptation.

Butterfly Garden: Experience the enchanting Butterfly Garden, where you can observe these delicate creatures up close as they flit about in a lush, tropical environment.

World Culture Halls: Discover artifacts and objects from various world cultures, shedding light on the customs, art, and traditions of diverse societies.

Special Exhibitions: The museum frequently hosts special exhibitions, so be sure to check what's on display during your visit for a unique experience.

Educational Programs: The Carnegie Museum of Natural History also offers a range of educational programs and events for visitors of all ages, including lectures, workshops, and interactive activities.

The museum's commitment to research and education is evident in its well-curated displays and interactive exhibits. It's an ideal destination for families, students, and anyone with a fascination for the natural world. As you explore the exhibits, you'll gain a deeper understanding of the Earth's history, biodiversity, and the wonders of our planet.

3. Take a ride on the Duquesne Incline.

Taking a ride on the Duquesne Incline in Pittsburgh is a delightful and iconic experience that offers breathtaking views of the city and its unique topography. The Duquesne Incline is not just a mode of transportation; it's a historic and scenic attraction that provides a memorable way to appreciate Pittsburgh's landscape.

As you ascend the incline, you'll be treated to spectacular panoramic views of the city's skyline, the three rivers (the Allegheny, Monongahela, and Ohio Rivers), and the many bridges that connect the various neighborhoods of Pittsburgh. The incline itself is an engineering marvel, and its century-old cable cars offer a charming and nostalgic journey.

Here's what you can expect when you take a ride on the Duquesne Incline:

Scenic Views: The incline cars travel along a steep hillside, giving you unobstructed views of the city, its landmarks, and the surrounding landscapes.

Historic Experience: The Duquesne Incline has been in operation since 1877 and is listed on the National Register of Historic Places. As you ride, you'll feel a sense of history and connection to the city's past.

Observation Deck: At the top, you'll find an observation deck with binoculars, allowing you to zoom in on specific points of interest and capture stunning photos.

Museum and Gift Shop: The upper station includes a small museum that provides additional insights into the history of the incline and Pittsburgh, as well as a gift shop where you can purchase souvenirs.

Historic Photos: Inside the upper station, you can also view historic photos that showcase the evolution of Pittsburgh over the years.

Photo Opportunities: The incline provides excellent opportunities for photographs, whether you're capturing the view from the observation deck or the incline cars themselves as they traverse the tracks.

Romantic or Relaxing: The Duquesne Incline is a popular spot for couples seeking a romantic outing, as well as individuals looking for a tranquil escape from the city's hustle and bustle.

It's important to note that the Duquesne Incline is a practical mode of transportation for those living in the neighborhood of Mount Washington, but it's also a beloved attraction for tourists and locals alike. The vistas from the incline are particularly stunning during sunset, offering a memorable experience that highlights the unique beauty of Pittsburgh.

4.Stroll through Phipps Conservatory and Botanical Gardens.

Strolling through Phipps Conservatory and Botanical Gardens in Pittsburgh is a tranquil and immersive experience that allows you to connect with nature, explore a wide variety of plant species, and enjoy the beauty of meticulously landscaped gardens. Phipps Conservatory is a historic and world-renowned institution that has been delighting visitors for over a century.

Here's what you can expect when you visit Phipps Conservatory and Botanical Gardens:

Lush Greenhouses: Phipps features several distinct greenhouses, each showcasing a different climate and plant collection. You can explore tropical, desert, and Mediterranean environments, among others, all under one roof.

Exquisite Flower Displays: Depending on the season, you'll encounter stunning flower displays that change throughout the year. From vibrant orchids to colorful tulips, Phipps is known for its captivating floral exhibitions.

Outdoor Gardens: Beyond the greenhouses, Phipps offers beautifully landscaped outdoor gardens. You can wander through themed gardens, such as the Japanese Courtyard Garden or the Rose Garden, and take in the scents and colors of various flowers and plants.

Sustainability and Conservation: Phipps is dedicated to sustainability and conservation efforts, which are incorporated into its displays and exhibits. You can learn about eco-friendly practices and sustainable gardening.

Educational Exhibits: The conservatory often hosts educational exhibits and displays related to botany, ecology, and environmental conservation. These exhibits provide valuable insights into the natural world and current environmental issues.

Butterfly Forest: If you visit during the Butterfly Forest exhibit (seasonal), you can witness hundreds of colorful butterflies in a lush and tropical environment.

Gift Shop: Phipps has a gift shop where you can find botanical-themed souvenirs, plants, and gardening books.

Café Phipps: If you need refreshments, Café Phipps offers a selection of light meals, snacks, and beverages in a lovely garden setting.

Educational Programs: The conservatory offers a range of educational programs, workshops, and classes for all ages, making it a great destination for families and students.

Photography Opportunities: Phipps is a photographer's paradise, with abundant opportunities to capture the beauty of plants, flowers, and gardens. Don't forget your camera!

Whether you're a botany enthusiast, nature lover, or simply seeking a peaceful and visually captivating experience, Phipps Conservatory and Botanical Gardens offers a refreshing and educational escape in the heart of Pittsburgh. It's a place to be inspired by the diversity and beauty of the natural world, no matter the season.

5.Attend a Pittsburgh Pirates baseball game at PNC Park.

Attending a Pittsburgh Pirates baseball game at PNC Park is a classic and enjoyable Pittsburgh experience, especially for sports fans. PNC Park, known for its picturesque setting along the Allegheny River and breathtaking views of the Pittsburgh skyline, offers an atmosphere that combines the excitement of baseball with the beauty of the city.

Here's what you can look forward to when attending a Pirates game at PNC Park:

Scenic Setting: PNC Park is often regarded as one of the most beautiful ballparks in the country. The views of the Roberto Clemente Bridge, the river, and the city's skyscrapers make for a stunning backdrop to the game.

Pittsburgh Pirates Baseball: Watch the Pirates in action as they take on their opponents in Major League Baseball. The team has a rich history, and the games are filled with excitement and the spirit of competition.

Family-Friendly Atmosphere: PNC Park is known for its family-friendly environment, making it an excellent destination for fans of all ages. The park offers kid-friendly activities and a designated family zone.

Delicious Ballpark Food: Indulge in classic ballpark fare like hot dogs, nachos, and peanuts, or explore the variety of food options available at PNC Park, including local Pittsburgh favorites.

Interactive Displays: Throughout the ballpark, you'll find interactive displays and exhibits celebrating the history of the Pirates and the sport of baseball.

Themed Nights: The Pirates often host themed nights and promotions, so you might catch a game on a night dedicated to a specific group or event.

Pirate Parrot: Keep an eye out for the team mascot, the Pirate Parrot, who provides entertainment and fun throughout the game.

Tailgating: Before the game, many fans partake in the time-honored tradition of tailgating in the parking lots surrounding the ballpark.

Postgame Fireworks: Some games feature postgame fireworks displays, adding a magical touch to the evening.

River Walk: After the game, take a leisurely walk along the North Shore Riverfront Park to enjoy the serene views of the river and city.

City Views: The best place to capture stunning photos of Pittsburgh's skyline is from the outfield stands of PNC Park, particularly during sunset.

Fan Engagement: The Pirates organization emphasizes fan engagement and community involvement, making your visit to a game not just about watching baseball but also about connecting with the city and its residents.

Attending a Pirates game at PNC Park offers a fantastic opportunity to enjoy baseball, savor delicious food, and soak up the beauty of Pittsburgh's waterfront. Whether you're a dedicated baseball fan or simply seeking a memorable outing, the experience at PNC Park is bound to be a hit.

6.Explore the National Aviary.

Exploring the National Aviary in Pittsburgh is a delightful and educational experience that allows you to connect with a diverse array of birds from around the world. As the nation's premier bird zoo, the National Aviary offers a unique opportunity to get up close to these fascinating creatures and learn more about their habitats and conservation efforts.

Here's what you can look forward to when visiting the National Aviary:

Indoor Habitats: The National Aviary features spacious indoor habitats that house a wide variety of birds, including colorful parrots, majestic raptors, and exotic toucans. You can observe these birds in settings that replicate their natural environments.

Outdoor Exhibits: Beyond indoor habitats, the National Aviary also offers outdoor exhibits where you can encounter species like penguins and flamingos. These outdoor spaces provide enriching experiences for both visitors and the birds.

Interactive Experiences: The Aviary offers several interactive experiences, such as feeding sessions and opportunities to interact with birds. You can get up close and personal with some of the residents and even participate in special encounters.

Special Exhibits: The Aviary often hosts special exhibits and events that focus on specific bird species, themes, or conservation efforts. These exhibits provide additional insights into the world of birds and the challenges they face.

Conservation Education: Education is a key focus of the National Aviary. You can learn about bird conservation efforts and how you can contribute to preserving avian species and their natural habitats.

Bird Shows: The Aviary hosts daily bird shows, where you can witness the intelligence and natural behaviors of various bird species. These shows are both entertaining and educational.

Café and Gift Shop: The facility includes a café where you can enjoy a meal or snack, as well as a gift shop where you can purchase bird-related souvenirs and gifts.

Photography Opportunities: The National Aviary provides ample opportunities for photography enthusiasts to capture the beauty and personality of the birds in their care.

Outdoor Garden: Explore the serene, landscaped gardens surrounding the Aviary, which provide a peaceful atmosphere for a leisurely stroll.

Family-Friendly: The National Aviary is a family-friendly destination, making it an excellent choice for visitors of all ages, from young children to adults.

Visiting the National Aviary is not only enjoyable but also contributes to the Aviary's mission of avian conservation and education. It's an ideal place to learn more about the diverse world of birds and appreciate their significance in the natural environment. Whether you're an avid bird enthusiast or simply seeking a unique and engaging outing, the National Aviary offers a memorable experience.

7. Visit the Carnegie Science Center.

Visiting the Carnegie Science Center in Pittsburgh is an enriching and interactive experience that offers a wide range of educational opportunities and hands-on exhibits for visitors of all ages. Whether you're a science enthusiast, a student, or simply looking for an engaging and fun outing, the Science Center has something for everyone.

Here's what you can look forward to when you visit the Carnegie Science Center:

Interactive Exhibits: The Science Center features a diverse array of interactive exhibits that cover various scientific disciplines, from astronomy and physics to biology and engineering. You can engage with exhibits that explain scientific concepts in a hands-on and entertaining manner.

Buhl Planetarium: Explore the Buhl Planetarium, which houses a state-of-the-art digital planetarium and offers captivating shows about the night sky, astronomy, and space exploration.

SportsWorks: SportsWorks, an exhibit within the Science Center, combines science with sports and offers fun and educational challenges related to physical fitness, reaction times, and more.

Roboworld: Discover the world of robotics and automation in Roboworld, where you can interact with robots and learn about their applications in various fields.

Live Demonstrations: Throughout the day, the Science Center hosts live science demonstrations that showcase scientific principles and phenomena. These presentations are both educational and entertaining.

Miniature Railroad & Village: The Miniature Railroad & Village is a beloved exhibit featuring intricate scale models of Pittsburgh and the surrounding region, offering a unique historical perspective.

Educational Programs: The Science Center offers educational programs, workshops, and summer camps for children and families. These programs provide opportunities to dive deeper into specific scientific topics.

3D Printing and Maker Space: Explore the 3D printing and maker space, where you can witness the process of creating three-dimensional objects using innovative technology.

Café and Gift Shop: The facility includes a café where you can grab a meal or snack, as well as a gift shop offering science-related souvenirs and educational items.

Observation Deck: The Carnegie Science Center boasts a scenic observation deck that provides breathtaking views of Pittsburgh and the surrounding area. It's an ideal spot for taking in the city's skyline.

Aquarium: In addition to its science exhibits, the Science Center also features a four-story-high, living, multi-story indoor rainforest, and a live coral reef.

Family-Friendly: The Carnegie Science Center is designed to be family-friendly, making it a great destination for visitors of all ages.

Visiting the Carnegie Science Center is not only enjoyable but also an opportunity to learn and engage with science, technology, and innovation. The interactive nature of the exhibits and the center's commitment to education make it a fantastic destination for anyone seeking to expand their knowledge and curiosity about the world of science.

8.Take a walk along the Three Rivers Heritage Trail.

Taking a walk along the Three Rivers Heritage Trail in Pittsburgh is a delightful outdoor experience that allows you to enjoy the city's natural beauty, riverfront views, and historical landmarks. The Three Rivers Heritage Trail is a network of scenic walking and biking paths that follow the banks of the three rivers in Pittsburgh: the Allegheny River, the Monongahela River, and the Ohio River.

Here's what you can expect when you walk along the Three Rivers Heritage Trail:

Scenic Beauty: The trail offers stunning views of Pittsburgh's rivers, bridges, and skyline. Whether you're walking along the banks of the Allegheny, Monongahela, or Ohio River, you'll have opportunities to capture breathtaking photographs.

Historic Landmarks: Along the trail, you'll encounter historical landmarks and markers that provide insights into Pittsburgh's industrial past and the role the rivers played in its development.

Bridges: Pittsburgh is known for its iconic bridges, and the trail offers great vantage points to admire these engineering marvels up close. You can also learn about the history and design of these bridges.

Parks and Green Spaces: The trail passes through or near several city parks and green spaces, providing opportunities for picnicking, relaxation, and wildlife observation.

Art and Sculptures: Keep an eye out for public art installations and sculptures that are scattered along the trail, adding to the cultural experience of your walk.

Fitness and Recreation: The Three Rivers Heritage Trail is suitable for walking, jogging, biking, and even rollerblading. It's a popular spot for outdoor enthusiasts and exercise.

Dog-Friendly: Many sections of the trail are dog-friendly, so you can bring your four-legged companion along for a scenic walk.

Events and Festivals: The trail is often used for community events, festivals, and outdoor concerts, so check the schedule for any happenings during your visit.

Connecting Neighborhoods: The trail connects various neighborhoods of Pittsburgh, making it a great way to explore the city and discover its different districts and cultures.

Riverfront Dining: Some sections of the trail feature riverfront restaurants and cafes, where you can stop for a meal or refreshments while enjoying the water views.

The Three Rivers Heritage Trail offers a mix of urban and natural landscapes, making it an ideal way to experience Pittsburgh's diverse scenery and culture. Whether you're interested in a leisurely walk, a long-distance bike ride, or simply a relaxing day by the river, this trail provides a unique and enjoyable opportunity to engage with the city's riverside charm.

9.Tour the Mattress Factory, a contemporary art museum.

Touring the Mattress Factory in Pittsburgh is a unique and immersive experience that allows you to explore contemporary art in a distinctive setting. This contemporary art museum is renowned for its site-specific installations and the opportunity to engage with art in unconventional ways.

Here's what you can expect when you visit the Mattress Factory:

Site-Specific Installations: The museum is dedicated to presenting site-specific installations created by artists from around the world. These installations often cover entire rooms or areas, providing an immersive and interactive experience.

Permanent Collections: The Mattress Factory has a permanent collection of works created by artists in residence. These works include a diverse range of mediums, from sculpture and sound art to mixed media and innovative technologies.

Artists in Residence: The museum hosts artists in residence, and you might have the chance to witness the creative process as artists work on new installations during your visit.

Interactive Art: Many of the installations are interactive, encouraging visitors to actively engage with the art. You can touch, explore, and even become a part of the artwork in some instances.

Outdoor Spaces: In addition to indoor exhibitions, the Mattress Factory features outdoor art installations and gardens. These areas offer additional opportunities to appreciate art in a natural setting.

Special Exhibitions: The museum frequently hosts special exhibitions and events, expanding the range of contemporary art experiences available to visitors.

Educational Programs: The Mattress Factory offers educational programs, workshops, and tours for visitors of all ages, making it an excellent destination for families and students.

Gift Shop: The museum has a gift shop where you can find art-related books, prints, and unique gifts.

Art Cafe: Enjoy light refreshments and a relaxing atmosphere at the on-site Art Cafe.

Photography Opportunities: The unusual and creative nature of the installations at the Mattress Factory provides fantastic opportunities for photography enthusiasts to capture art in a unique way.

The Mattress Factory is a place to explore the boundaries of contemporary art and experience creativity in unconventional forms. Whether you're a dedicated art enthusiast, a lover of experimental art, or simply looking for a different kind of cultural experience, the museum offers an opportunity to engage with art that challenges and inspires.

10.Experience the historic Strip District's food markets.

Experiencing the historic Strip District's food markets in Pittsburgh is a culinary adventure like no other. The Strip District, located just northeast of downtown Pittsburgh, is known for its vibrant and diverse food scene, offering an array of fresh produce, specialty foods, international cuisine, and local delights. Here's what you can look forward to when you explore the Strip District's food markets:

Fresh Produce: The markets in the Strip District are brimming with fresh fruits, vegetables, and herbs. It's a great place to find locally sourced and seasonal produce.

International Flavors: You'll discover a diverse range of international foods, from Italian and Mediterranean to Asian, Mexican, and Eastern European specialties. The Strip District is a melting pot of flavors.

Meat and Seafood: Butcher shops and seafood markets in the area provide top-quality cuts of meat, sausages, and fresh seafood for your culinary adventures.

Cheese and Dairy: Cheese lovers will be delighted by the selection of cheeses and dairy products available, including artisanal and imported varieties.

Bakeries: There are numerous bakeries in the Strip District where you can find freshly baked bread, pastries, cookies, and other baked goods.

Coffee and Tea: Specialty coffee shops and tea stores offer a wide selection of beverages, beans, and teas from around the world.

Spices and Herbs: Spice shops carry an extensive range of spices, herbs, and seasonings, allowing you to explore new flavors in your cooking.

Sweets and Confections: Satiate your sweet tooth with chocolates, candies, and confections from local chocolatiers and sweet shops.

Street Food: As you explore the Strip District, you'll come across food vendors and street food carts offering delicious snacks, sandwiches, and ethnic dishes.

Historic Atmosphere: The Strip District's historic buildings and markets provide a unique and charming backdrop for your culinary journey. Many of the markets have been around for generations.

Artisanal Foods: You can discover artisanal and gourmet foods, from olive oils and vinegars to unique sauces and jams, which make for great souvenirs or gifts.

Antique and Specialty Shops: In addition to food markets, the Strip District features antique shops, boutiques, and specialty stores where you can find one-of-a-kind items and gifts.

Weekend Markets: On weekends, the area comes alive with outdoor markets and vendors, selling everything from crafts to clothing and more.

Food Tours: Consider joining a guided food tour of the Strip District to get an insider's perspective and taste your way through the area.

Visiting the Strip District's food markets is not just a culinary experience; it's a cultural and historical immersion into Pittsburgh's rich and diverse heritage. It's an opportunity to explore unique flavors, shop for fresh ingredients, and enjoy a lively atmosphere in a neighborhood that has been at the heart of the city's food culture for over a century.

11.Explore the Pittsburgh Zoo & PPG Aquarium.

Exploring the Pittsburgh Zoo & PPG Aquarium is an exciting and educational adventure that allows you to connect with a diverse range of animal species from around the world. This dynamic zoo and aquarium complex provides a fun and engaging experience for visitors of all ages.

Here's what you can look forward to when you visit the Pittsburgh Zoo & PPG Aquarium:

Animal Exhibits: The zoo features numerous animal exhibits, from African savannahs and rainforests to polar environments and aquatic habitats. You can observe a variety of animals, including lions, tigers, elephants, penguins, sea otters, sharks, and more.

Aquatic Life: The PPG Aquarium, part of the complex, offers the opportunity to explore aquatic ecosystems and observe marine life, including sea turtles, jellyfish, and colorful fish.

Conservation Efforts: The zoo is actively involved in conservation efforts and educational programs to raise awareness about endangered species and the importance of preserving natural habitats.

Interactive Experiences: The zoo provides interactive and hands-on experiences for visitors, including opportunities to feed giraffes, pet certain animals, and learn about animal behavior and conservation.

Educational Programs: The Pittsburgh Zoo & PPG Aquarium offers educational programs, camps, and workshops for children and adults. These programs provide insights into animal biology, conservation, and environmental stewardship.

Special Exhibits: The complex hosts special exhibits and events throughout the year, offering fresh perspectives and exciting attractions.

Family-Friendly: The zoo is family-friendly and caters to children of all ages, with play areas and kid-focused exhibits.

Beautiful Grounds: In addition to animal exhibits, the zoo features beautifully landscaped grounds and gardens, making it a lovely place for a leisurely walk or picnic.

Dining Options: The complex includes dining facilities and cafes where you can enjoy a meal or snack while overlooking some of the animal habitats.

Photography Opportunities: The diverse collection of animals and beautiful habitats provides ample opportunities for photography enthusiasts to capture the beauty of the natural world.

Conservation Initiatives: The Pittsburgh Zoo & PPG Aquarium is actively involved in various conservation initiatives and supports global efforts to protect endangered species and their habitats.

Membership: Consider becoming a member of the zoo to enjoy benefits like free admission, special events, and more.

Visiting the Pittsburgh Zoo & PPG Aquarium is not just an enjoyable outing; it's also an opportunity to appreciate the world's biodiversity and learn about the critical role zoos and aquariums play in wildlife conservation. Whether you're passionate about animals, a nature enthusiast, or seeking a family-friendly adventure, the complex offers a memorable and educational experience.

12. Take a cruise on the Gateway Clipper Fleet.

Taking a cruise on the Gateway Clipper Fleet in Pittsburgh is a relaxing and scenic way to experience the city from the water. The Gateway Clipper Fleet offers a variety of cruises, each providing a unique perspective on Pittsburgh's stunning riverfront and iconic landmarks.

Here's what you can look forward to when you take a cruise on the Gateway Clipper Fleet:

Scenic Views: Enjoy panoramic views of Pittsburgh's skyline and its numerous bridges as you cruise along the city's three rivers—the Allegheny, Monongahela, and Ohio.

Narrated Tours: Most Gateway Clipper cruises feature informative and entertaining narration about the history, culture, and landmarks of Pittsburgh. Learn about the city's industrial past, vibrant present, and exciting future.

Specialty Cruises: The Gateway Clipper Fleet offers a variety of specialty cruises, including sightseeing cruises, dinner cruises, brunch cruises, and themed cruises. You can choose the one that best suits your interests and preferences.

Live Entertainment: Some cruises feature live music, DJs, or other forms of entertainment to enhance the experience.

Historic Landmarks: Cruise past and get close-up views of iconic Pittsburgh landmarks like Point State Park, Heinz Field (home of the Pittsburgh Steelers), PNC Park (home of the Pittsburgh Pirates), and more.

Bridges: Pittsburgh is famous for its numerous bridges, and a cruise provides an excellent opportunity to appreciate their architectural beauty and understand their significance in the city's history.

Relaxation: Enjoy a leisurely cruise on the water, whether you're taking in the sights from the open decks or relaxing in the climate-controlled indoor spaces.

Culinary Delights: On dinner and brunch cruises, you can savor a meal while enjoying the picturesque views. The menus typically feature a variety of dining options to suit your taste.

Photography Opportunities: The serene river setting offers excellent opportunities for photographers to capture Pittsburgh's skyline and riverfront.

Events and Parties: The Gateway Clipper Fleet hosts special events, parties, and celebrations, including weddings, corporate gatherings, and private charters.

Family-Friendly: Many of the cruises are family-friendly, making them a great outing for visitors of all ages.

Fireworks Cruises: During special events or holidays, the Gateway Clipper Fleet offers fireworks cruises, providing a front-row seat to impressive pyrotechnic displays over the rivers.

Taking a cruise on the Gateway Clipper Fleet is a memorable and enjoyable way to explore the city of Pittsburgh, whether you're a tourist or a local looking for a unique perspective on the city you love. The tranquil waterways and scenic beauty of the Three Rivers provide a wonderful backdrop for an unforgettable experience.

13.Discover the history of the Heinz History Center.

The Senator John Heinz History Center, located in Pittsburgh, Pennsylvania, is the largest history museum in the state and one of the most prominent history museums in the United States. The History Center's mission is to preserve and showcase the history of Western Pennsylvania and its impact on the nation and the world. Here's a look at the history of this remarkable institution:

Travel to Pittsburgh Pennsylvania

Early Origins: The Heinz History Center has its roots in the Historical Society of Western Pennsylvania, which was founded in 1879. The society was dedicated to preserving and promoting the region's history and cultural heritage.

Name Change: In 1996, the Historical Society underwent a significant transformation. The organization was renamed the Senator John Heinz Pittsburgh Regional History Center to honor the memory of U.S. Senator John Heinz, who was a champion of the region's heritage and a prominent figure in Pennsylvania politics.

New Home: The History Center moved to its current location in Pittsburgh's Strip District in 1996, where it occupies a historic warehouse that was repurposed for its present use. The building itself is an integral part of Pittsburgh's industrial past.

Exhibits and Collections: The History Center's extensive collection includes over 100,000 artifacts, documents, and photographs, spanning a wide range of topics related to Western Pennsylvania's history, from the prehistoric era to the present day.

Main Exhibit: One of the center's main exhibits, "Pittsburgh: A Tradition of Innovation," explores the region's rich history of innovation, invention, and industrial prowess. It highlights achievements in fields like manufacturing, technology, and medicine.

Sports Museum: The Western Pennsylvania Sports Museum, which is part of the History Center, celebrates the region's love of sports and its contributions to the world of athletics. It features memorabilia, interactive displays, and exhibits dedicated to the achievements of Western Pennsylvania athletes.

Education and Outreach: The History Center is actively involved in education and outreach programs, including school tours, workshops, and special events for students, teachers, and the public.

Historical Research: The History Center provides resources and support for historical research, making it a valuable destination for scholars and researchers interested in the history of the region.

Community Engagement: The History Center is deeply engaged with the local community, offering a variety of programs and events that celebrate Pittsburgh's history and heritage.

The Heinz History Center stands as a testament to the rich and diverse history of Western Pennsylvania and its significant impact on the development of the United States. It offers visitors a chance to explore the region's industrial, cultural, and social history and to gain a deeper understanding of its enduring contributions to American life.

14. Visit Fallingwater, Frank Lloyd Wright's masterpiece

Fallingwater, designed by the renowned architect Frank Lloyd Wright, is one of the most iconic architectural masterpieces in the United States. Located in the Laurel Highlands of southwestern Pennsylvania, Fallingwater is celebrated for its innovative design and integration with the natural landscape. Here's what you can expect when you visit this architectural gem:

Architectural Marvel: Fallingwater is a prime example of Frank Lloyd Wright's organic architecture philosophy, where the building is harmoniously integrated with the surrounding environment. It is known for its cantilevered terraces, stone walls, and naturalistic design.

Natural Setting: The house is perched above a waterfall on Bear Run, surrounded by a lush forest. The design seamlessly incorporates the waterfall and the rocky terrain into the structure.

Guided Tours: Visits to Fallingwater are guided tours, allowing you to gain a deeper understanding of the architectural principles behind the house and the story of its creation.

Interior Exploration: The tour provides access to the interior spaces, where you can admire the unique design elements, including built-in furniture, art, and extensive use of glass to connect with the outdoors.

Photography Opportunities: The house and its picturesque setting offer fantastic photo opportunities, capturing the beauty of the architecture against the backdrop of the natural surroundings.

Visitor Center: Fallingwater has a visitor center that offers additional information about the house and the architect, as well as a cafe and gift shop where you can find books, souvenirs, and architectural-related items.

Educational Programs: Fallingwater offers educational programs and workshops for those interested in exploring architectural and design concepts.

Conservation: The Western Pennsylvania Conservancy, which operates Fallingwater, is dedicated to the preservation of the property and its natural surroundings.

Advance Reservations: Due to the popularity of Fallingwater, it's advisable to make advance reservations for tours, as the number of visitors is limited to preserve the experience.

Visiting Fallingwater is a unique and enriching experience, providing insight into the genius of Frank Lloyd Wright and the timeless appeal of his architecture. It's an opportunity to appreciate the fusion of art and nature in a way that continues to inspire architects and admirers of design worldwide.

15.Attend a Pittsburgh Steelers football game at Heinz Field.

Attending a Pittsburgh Steelers football game at Heinz Field is an electrifying and quintessentially Pittsburgh experience for sports enthusiasts. Heinz Field, the iconic home of the Pittsburgh Steelers, is a hub of passion, tradition, and excitement. Here's what you can look forward to when you attend a game:

Game Day Atmosphere: Heinz Field boasts a lively and electric atmosphere on game days. The sea of black and gold-clad fans, known as "Steelers Nation," creates an unparalleled sense of community and team spirit.

Terrible Towels: The Terrible Towel is a cherished symbol of Steelers fandom. Wave your Terrible Towel with pride to show your support for the team and join in the iconic game-day tradition.

Tailgating: Heinz Field's parking lots come alive with tailgating festivities before the game. Join fellow fans in pre-game celebrations that often include grilling, music, games, and camaraderie.

Stadium Amenities: Inside the stadium, you'll find a range of amenities, including a variety of food and beverage options, team stores, and interactive exhibits dedicated to the Steelers' history.

Great Views: Heinz Field offers excellent sightlines, ensuring that fans have a great view of the action on the field. The stadium's design also provides views of the city skyline and the nearby rivers.

Pregame Traditions: Don't miss out on pregame traditions, such as the playing of "Renegade" and the roaring crowd as the team takes the field.

Intense Rivalries: The Steelers have a number of intense rivalries in the NFL, including matchups with the Baltimore Ravens and the Cincinnati Bengals. These games are especially spirited.

Loyal Fan Base: Pittsburgh Steelers fans are known for their loyalty and passionate support of the team. Attending a game allows you to connect with fans from all walks of life who share a deep love for the team.

Championship Legacy: The Pittsburgh Steelers have a storied history, with multiple Super Bowl championships to their name. The walls of Heinz Field are adorned with reminders of the team's successful history.

Unique Design: The stadium's unique open-end design allows the elements to play a role in the game. Be prepared for changing weather conditions, as Pittsburgh's climate can vary greatly from game to game.

Postgame Celebrations: After a Steelers victory, you can join in postgame celebrations in the stands or participate in the city-wide excitement of another successful game.

Attending a Pittsburgh Steelers game at Heinz Field is an exhilarating experience that provides a profound sense of community, pride, and shared enthusiasm for the team. Whether you're a lifelong fan or a first-time visitor, the atmosphere, traditions, and passionate fan base make it a must-see event for anyone visiting Pittsburgh during football season.

16.Explore the ToonSeum, a museum dedicated to comics and cartoons.

The ToonSeum, located in Pittsburgh, is a delightful and unique museum dedicated to comics, cartoons, and the art of visual storytelling. This museum

Public Art: As you walk along the riverfront, you'll encounter various sculptures and art installations, which add an artistic element to the outdoor experience.

Fountains and Water Features: The park includes fountains and water features that contribute to the relaxing ambiance and provide an opportunity for contemplation.

Green Spaces: There are open green spaces in the park where you can sit, have a picnic, or simply relax while taking in the views.

Bridges: The North Shore Riverfront Park is known for its excellent views of Pittsburgh's many bridges, including the colorful lights of the Rachel Carson Bridge.

Cultural Attractions: The park is adjacent to several cultural attractions, such as the Andy Warhol Museum, the Mattress Factory, and the National Aviary, making it an ideal starting point for a day of exploration.

Events and Festivals: Throughout the year, the park hosts various events and festivals, ranging from outdoor concerts to community gatherings. Check the schedule for any happenings during your visit.

Family-Friendly: The park is family-friendly and offers play areas for children, making it a great destination for families.

Water Activities: If you're interested in water activities, you can also find kayak rentals and riverboat tours nearby.

Taking a walk along the North Shore Riverfront Park is a rejuvenating and visually stimulating experience, allowing you to appreciate Pittsburgh's natural beauty, riverfront culture, and urban charm. Whether you're a local looking for a peaceful escape or a visitor exploring the city, this park offers a memorable way to engage with the rivers that have played a central role in Pittsburgh's history and development.

Quiet Retreat: Schenley Park is an ideal place for a quiet retreat and a leisurely drive, allowing you to unwind while staying close to the city.

Picnicking: The park has numerous picnic areas where you can stop for a meal or a snack. It's an excellent spot for a picnic with a view.

Family-Friendly: Schenley Park is family-friendly, and you'll often see families enjoying the outdoors and playing in the grassy areas.

Fall Foliage: During the fall, the park's foliage comes alive with vibrant colors, making it an ideal time for a scenic drive to enjoy the autumn beauty.

Taking a drive through Schenley Park is a serene and rejuvenating experience that allows you to connect with nature without leaving the city limits. It's a place where you can escape the urban environment and immerse yourself in the tranquility of nature while still enjoying the convenience of Pittsburgh's amenities.

18.Take a walk along the North Shore Riverfront Park.

Taking a walk along the North Shore Riverfront Park in Pittsburgh is a delightful way to experience the city's stunning riverfront and take in some of its most iconic landmarks. The park is situated on the north shore of the Allegheny River and offers a blend of natural beauty, recreational opportunities, and breathtaking views. Here's what you can expect when you enjoy a walk in this picturesque park:

Riverfront Beauty: The North Shore Riverfront Park is known for its scenic beauty, offering unobstructed views of the Allegheny River and the city skyline. The park's design seamlessly integrates nature with urban surroundings.

Trail System: The park features a well-maintained trail system that is ideal for walking, jogging, and biking. You can explore the riverfront at your own pace, taking in the serene atmosphere and enjoying the river breeze.

City Skyline: The park's location provides excellent views of Pittsburgh's iconic skyline, including notable landmarks like PNC Park, Heinz Field, and the Roberto Clemente Bridge.

contemporary graphic novels. Whether you're an avid comic book reader, a fan of animation, or simply curious about the impact of visual storytelling, the ToonSeum offers an engaging and insightful experience.

17.Enjoy a scenic drive through Schenley Park.

Taking a scenic drive through Schenley Park in Pittsburgh is a wonderful way to experience the natural beauty and greenery of the city. Schenley Park, one of the city's most beloved green spaces, offers a peaceful escape from the urban hustle and bustle. Here's what you can expect when you enjoy a drive through Schenley Park:

Lush Landscapes: Schenley Park is characterized by its lush landscapes, including woodlands, open fields, gardens, and meandering pathways. The park's 456 acres offer a diverse range of natural beauty.

Serpentine Drive: The park features a picturesque road called Serpentine Drive, which winds through the heart of the park. The scenic drive allows you to explore the park's various sections at a leisurely pace.

Panoramic Views: Along the drive, you'll encounter numerous overlooks and vantage points that provide panoramic views of Pittsburgh's skyline, the surrounding hills, and Panther Hollow Lake.

Recreational Areas: Schenley Park is home to various recreational areas, including walking and jogging paths, picnic spots, and sports fields. You'll see people enjoying activities like frisbee, soccer, and birdwatching.

Phipps Conservatory: Near the park's entrance, you can visit the Phipps Conservatory and Botanical Gardens, known for its stunning plant collections and unique greenhouse environments.

Historical Landmarks: Keep an eye out for historical landmarks and sculptures, including the Christopher Columbus monument, which adds to the park's charm.

Botanical Gardens: The park is home to lovely botanical gardens, offering a tranquil setting for a relaxing drive. The gardens are especially vibrant in spring and summer.

celebrates the rich history and cultural significance of comics and cartoons, making it an engaging destination for comic enthusiasts, art lovers, and families. Here's what you can expect when you explore the ToonSeum:

Exhibits: The ToonSeum features a rotating selection of exhibits that showcase various aspects of comics and cartoons. These exhibits may focus on the works of specific artists, iconic characters, or the evolution of the medium.

Comic Art: The museum's collections include original comic art, comic books, graphic novels, and other comic-related artifacts. You can see original drawings, sketches, and comic book covers.

Cartoon History: Learn about the history of cartoons and their cultural impact through informative displays and interactive exhibits.

Local and International Artists: The ToonSeum highlights the work of both local and international comic artists and cartoonists, offering insights into their creative processes.

Educational Programs: The museum hosts educational programs, workshops, and events for all ages. These programs provide opportunities to learn more about the art of comics and storytelling.

Comic Creation: Some exhibits and events may focus on the process of creating comics, offering visitors a chance to explore their own creative talents.

Special Events: The ToonSeum often hosts special events, including book signings, lectures, and film screenings related to comics and cartoons.

Gift Shop: The museum's gift shop offers a range of comic books, graphic novels, art prints, and unique comic-related items for purchase.

Family-Friendly: The ToonSeum is a family-friendly destination, with exhibits and programs suitable for visitors of all ages.

Pop Culture: Explore the connections between comics, cartoons, and popular culture, as the museum showcases how these art forms have influenced and reflected the broader cultural landscape.

Visiting the ToonSeum is an opportunity to appreciate the creativity and storytelling prowess of the comic and cartoon world. It's a museum that embraces the art form's diversity and evolution, from classic comic strips to

19. Visit the Soldiers & Sailors Memorial Hall and Museum.

The Soldiers & Sailors Memorial Hall and Museum in Pittsburgh is a prestigious institution that pays tribute to the men and women who have served in the United States military. It is a place of historical significance and a center for education and reflection on the nation's military history. Here's what you can expect when you visit this important memorial and museum:

Historical Significance: The Soldiers & Sailors Memorial Hall and Museum was established to honor the sacrifices of those who served in the military, particularly those from Western Pennsylvania. The neoclassical building itself is an architectural gem and was dedicated in 1910 as a memorial to veterans.

Exhibits: The museum houses an extensive collection of artifacts, documents, and memorabilia related to the military. The exhibits cover a wide range of military conflicts, including the Civil War, World War I, World War II, the Korean War, the Vietnam War, and more.

Civil War Hall: The Civil War Hall is a standout exhibit within the museum, featuring an impressive collection of Civil War artifacts, including uniforms, weapons, and flags. The exhibit offers insights into the region's significant role in the Civil War.

Educational Programs: The museum offers educational programs, lectures, and workshops that help visitors understand the history and significance of the various military conflicts. These programs are suitable for all ages.

Memorial Auditorium: The Memorial Auditorium is a stunning space that hosts events, concerts, and gatherings. It features a grand interior with a large military mural and stained glass windows.

Veterans' Services: The Soldiers & Sailors Memorial Hall and Museum provides services and resources for veterans, including assistance with benefits and support for veterans' organizations.

Honoring Veterans: The institution is a place to pay respect to veterans, and it often hosts ceremonies and memorial events to honor those who have served in the military.

Research Opportunities: If you're interested in military history or genealogy, the museum offers access to its archives and research materials.

Family-Friendly: The museum is family-friendly, and its educational programs are suitable for children and young adults, making it a valuable resource for teaching the younger generation about military history.

Gift Shop: The museum has a gift shop where you can find military-related books, souvenirs, and memorabilia.

Visiting the Soldiers & Sailors Memorial Hall and Museum is a way to connect with the rich military history of the United States and Western Pennsylvania, paying tribute to the men and women who have made tremendous sacrifices in service to their country. It's a place for reflection, education, and a deep appreciation of the nation's military heritage.

20.Explore Randyland, a colorful art installation in the North Side.

Randyland, located in the North Side neighborhood of Pittsburgh, is a vibrant and whimsical art installation that has captured the hearts of both locals and visitors. This colorful wonderland, created by artist Randy Gilson, is a true testament to the power of creativity and the transformative nature of art. Here's what you can expect when you explore Randyland:

Colorful Oasis: Randyland is a burst of color and creativity that stands in stark contrast to the surrounding urban environment. As soon as you enter, you'll be greeted by a kaleidoscope of bright and cheerful hues.

Outdoor Gallery: The installation is an open-air art gallery that extends across a house and its adjoining courtyard. Every inch is adorned with imaginative artwork, sculptures, and eclectic decorations.

Unique Artwork: Randyland features a wide variety of artwork, from hand-painted signs to murals, sculptures, mosaics, and found-object art. Each piece tells a story or conveys a message.

Interactive Elements: Visitors are encouraged to interact with the art. You can often find paints and brushes on hand for those who want to leave their mark on the ever-evolving artwork.

Community Engagement: Randy Gilson, the artist behind Randyland, is known for his warm and welcoming personality. He's often on-site to greet visitors and share stories about his art and the neighborhood's history.

Photography Paradise: The vivid colors and whimsical designs make Randyland a popular spot for photographers and Instagram enthusiasts. It's an excellent place to capture imaginative and joyful photos.

Positive Vibes: Randyland exudes a spirit of positivity and inclusivity. The art reflects themes of love, unity, and community, making it a heartwarming destination.

Free Admission: Entrance to Randyland is free, and the site operates on a donation basis, so visitors are encouraged to contribute to support the ongoing creation and maintenance of this art oasis.

Events and Performances: The space occasionally hosts events, performances, and live music, adding to the dynamic and creative atmosphere.

Community Impact: Randyland has played a vital role in revitalizing the North Side neighborhood, helping to transform an area once marred by blight into a place of artistic vibrancy.

Exploring Randyland is a unique and uplifting experience that celebrates the power of art and its ability to bring communities together. It's a must-visit for anyone looking to be inspired, delighted, and immersed in a world of boundless creativity.

21.Attend a concert at Stage AE.

Attending a concert at Stage AE in Pittsburgh is a fantastic way to enjoy live music in a vibrant and contemporary setting. Stage AE, located on the city's North Shore, is a popular concert venue known for hosting a wide range of musical acts, from up-and-coming bands to well-established artists. Here's what you can expect when you attend a concert at Stage AE:

Versatile Venue: Stage AE is a versatile concert venue with both indoor and outdoor stages, offering flexibility for various types of performances and events.

Outdoor Amphitheater: The outdoor stage provides an open-air concert experience during the warmer months. It has a capacity of several thousand attendees and features great views of the Pittsburgh skyline.

Indoor Stage: The indoor stage is an intimate space with a smaller capacity, providing an up-close and personal concert experience. It's used for concerts year-round.

Diverse Acts: Stage AE hosts a diverse lineup of musical acts, including rock, pop, hip-hop, country, electronic, and indie artists. You can catch performances from both local and nationally recognized musicians.

Standing Room: Most concerts at Stage AE offer a standing room experience, allowing you to get close to the stage and immerse yourself in the music.

Balcony Area: There is a balcony area with seating for those who prefer a more relaxed vantage point to enjoy the show.

Full-Service Bar: The venue features a full-service bar with a selection of beverages, making it easy to enjoy your favorite drinks during the concert.

Sound and Lighting: Stage AE is known for its excellent sound and lighting systems, ensuring a top-notch concert experience for attendees.

Concert Atmosphere: The energy and atmosphere at Stage AE are always electric, with passionate fans coming together to celebrate their favorite artists.

Convenient Location: The venue is conveniently located on the North Shore, making it easily accessible from various parts of the city.

Pre- and Post-Show Dining: The North Shore area offers a variety of dining options, so you can enjoy a meal or drinks before or after the concert.

Diverse Events: In addition to concerts, Stage AE hosts a range of other events, including festivals, comedy shows, and private gatherings.

Attending a concert at Stage AE is an unforgettable experience, whether you're a die-hard music fan or simply looking to enjoy a live performance in a lively and dynamic setting. The venue's versatility, excellent acoustics, and commitment to providing exceptional entertainment make it a beloved destination for concertgoers in Pittsburgh.

22. Experience the historic Kennywood amusement park.

Kennywood amusement park, located in West Mifflin, just outside of Pittsburgh, is a historic and beloved destination for family fun and thrilling rides. Established in 1898, Kennywood is one of the oldest amusement parks in the United States, known for its classic charm, iconic rides, and exciting attractions. Here's what you can expect when you experience the historic Kennywood amusement park:

Classic Rides: Kennywood boasts a mix of classic and modern rides, making it a delightful destination for visitors of all ages. Some classic rides have been entertaining guests for generations, preserving the park's nostalgic charm.

Iconic Wooden Coasters: The park is famous for its wooden roller coasters, including The Racer and The Thunderbolt. These rides offer an exhilarating and timeless amusement park experience.

Modern Thrill Rides: Kennywood has introduced modern thrill rides to cater to adrenaline enthusiasts. These include the Phantom's Revenge, Sky Rocket, and the Steel Curtain roller coaster, offering a heart-pounding experience.

Family-Friendly Attractions: Kennywood provides a range of family-friendly rides and attractions, including the Jack Rabbit, Noah's Ark, and the merry-go-round, allowing guests of all ages to enjoy the park.

Kiddieland: The park has a dedicated area called Kiddieland, featuring gentle rides and attractions designed for young children.

Entertainment: Throughout the season, Kennywood offers live entertainment, including shows, music, and special events.

Unique Dining: The park features unique dining options, from classic amusement park fare to local favorites like Potato Patch fries. Don't forget to try the famous Potato Patch fries with various toppings.

Picnic Groves: Kennywood offers picnic groves for visitors to enjoy a meal in a relaxed outdoor setting.

Seasonal Events: The park hosts special events during different seasons, such as Halloween-themed "Phantom Fright Nights" and holiday celebrations during the winter.

Character Meet and Greets: Meet and greet popular characters, including those from the Peanuts comic strip.

Historical Significance: Kennywood has a rich history and is recognized as a National Historic Landmark, making it a unique and culturally significant amusement park.

Retro Fun: Visitors appreciate the park's classic, retro atmosphere, transporting them to a bygone era of amusement parks.

Experiencing Kennywood amusement park is a nostalgic and entertaining journey through the world of classic and modern amusements. It's a family-friendly destination that offers a blend of old-world charm and thrilling adventures, making it a cherished place for generations of visitors to create lasting memories.

23. Visit the Pittsburgh Center for the Arts.

The Pittsburgh Center for the Arts, also known as PCA, was an important cultural institution in Pittsburgh dedicated to the promotion of the visual arts. However, as of my last knowledge update in September 2021, the Pittsburgh Center for the Arts had experienced some changes. Here's a general overview of what you might have expected when visiting PCA:

Exhibitions: PCA regularly hosted a variety of art exhibitions featuring works by local, national, and international artists. These exhibitions often showcased a wide range of artistic mediums, styles, and themes.

Local Artist Support: The center played a significant role in supporting and promoting local artists by providing exhibition opportunities, studio space, and resources for artists to develop their craft.

Educational Programs: PCA offered art classes, workshops, and educational programs for people of all ages and skill levels. These programs aimed to nurture artistic talent and creativity within the community.

Community Engagement: The center encouraged community engagement and involvement in the arts by organizing events, lectures, and discussions related to visual arts and culture.

Gallery Spaces: PCA had gallery spaces where visitors could explore and appreciate contemporary and traditional art forms.

Art Sales: Some exhibitions and events included opportunities to purchase art, supporting local artists and the center's mission.

Artistic Diversity: The center celebrated artistic diversity, showcasing a wide array of art forms, from painting and sculpture to new media and digital art.

Please note that the status and operations of cultural institutions like the Pittsburgh Center for the Arts may change over time.

24.Explore the South Side Works, a shopping and entertainment district.

South Side Works is a vibrant shopping and entertainment district located in the South Side neighborhood of Pittsburgh. This dynamic area offers a mix of retail shops, dining options, entertainment venues, and cultural attractions. Here's what you can expect when you explore South Side Works:

Retail Shopping: South Side Works features a variety of retail shops and boutiques where you can find clothing, accessories, home goods, and more. It's a great place to shop for unique and stylish items.

Dining Options: The district offers a wide range of dining options, from casual eateries to upscale restaurants. You can enjoy a diverse selection of cuisines, including American, Italian, Mexican, and more.

Entertainment Venues: South Side Works is known for its entertainment options, including a multiplex cinema where you can catch the latest films. It's a great spot for a movie night.

Nightlife: In the evenings, the South Side neighborhood comes alive with a vibrant nightlife scene. You'll find bars, pubs, and clubs that offer a variety of music and entertainment.

Waterfront Location: The district's location along the Monongahela River provides picturesque views and the opportunity for scenic riverside walks.

Cultural Attractions: South Side Works is home to the Pittsburgh Ballet Theatre, which offers dance performances and cultural events throughout the year. Be sure to check the schedule for any upcoming shows or productions.

Special Events: The district occasionally hosts special events, including art shows, festivals, and outdoor concerts. These events add to the lively and social atmosphere.

Fitness and Wellness: You'll also find fitness studios and wellness centers in the area, offering opportunities for physical activity and self-care.

Convenient Location: South Side Works is conveniently located just a short drive or walk from downtown Pittsburgh, making it easily accessible to both residents and visitors.

Scenic Views: Whether you're walking along the riverfront or dining at a restaurant with outdoor seating, you can enjoy scenic views of the river, bridges, and the city skyline.

Shopping Centers: In addition to the South Side Works complex, the South Side neighborhood offers several other shopping centers and street shopping options, giving you even more choices for retail therapy.

South Side Works is a bustling and diverse district that provides a mix of entertainment, shopping, dining, and cultural experiences. Whether you're looking for a stylish shopping spree, a delicious meal, or a night on the town, South Side Works has something for everyone to enjoy.

25.Attend a show at the Benedum Center for the Performing Arts.

The Benedum Center for the Performing Arts, located in the heart of Pittsburgh's Cultural District, is a magnificent venue for experiencing a wide range of live performances. This historic theater is renowned for hosting Broadway productions, musicals, concerts, ballets, and other cultural events. Here's what you can expect when you attend a show at the Benedum Center:

Travel to Pittsburgh Pennsylvania

Elegant Venue: The Benedum Center is a beautifully restored and grand historic theater, featuring ornate architecture, chandeliers, and a lavish interior that adds to the overall theater experience.

Broadway Productions: The theater is famous for hosting touring Broadway productions, including popular musicals, classic plays, and contemporary shows.

Musical Performances: In addition to Broadway, the Benedum Center welcomes a diverse range of musical acts, including orchestral concerts, rock bands, and solo artists.

Ballet and Dance: The venue is home to the Pittsburgh Ballet Theatre, making it a hub for ballet performances and dance events. You can enjoy classical and contemporary ballet productions.

Opera and Theater: Opera and dramatic performances are also regularly featured at the Benedum Center, with a focus on showcasing the arts in Pittsburgh.

Acoustic Excellence: The theater's exceptional acoustics and intimate setting make it an ideal place to enjoy live performances, ensuring that you hear every note and appreciate the artistry of the performers.

Pre-Show and Intermission: The Benedum Center provides ample space in its lobby and lounges for patrons to gather before the show and during intermission, allowing you to socialize and enjoy refreshments.

Accessible Location: The theater is conveniently situated in Pittsburgh's Cultural District, making it easily accessible by foot, public transportation, and car. There are many restaurants and shops nearby.

Special Events: The venue hosts special events and galas, often associated with performances, providing a chance for social engagement and support for the arts.

Cultural Hub: The Benedum Center contributes to Pittsburgh's status as a cultural hub and plays a pivotal role in the city's arts and entertainment scene.

Before attending a show at the Benedum Center, be sure to check the schedule and purchase tickets in advance, as popular shows can sell out quickly. Whether you're a fan of Broadway, live music, ballet, or theater, the Benedum Center offers a sophisticated and memorable setting for a night of cultural entertainment.

26.Go kayaking or paddleboarding on the city's rivers.

Exploring Pittsburgh's rivers by kayaking or paddleboarding is a wonderful way to experience the city from a different perspective and enjoy the natural beauty of the waterways. Here's what you can expect when you go kayaking or paddleboarding on the city's rivers:

Scenic Views: Paddling on the rivers offers stunning views of Pittsburgh's skyline, bridges, and surrounding greenery. You'll see the city from a unique vantage point and appreciate its beauty.

River Options: Pittsburgh is situated at the confluence of the Allegheny, Monongahela, and Ohio Rivers. You can choose to paddle on any of these rivers, each offering its own charm and views.

Rental Options: Several outfitters and rental shops in the area provide kayaks, paddleboards, and all necessary equipment for rent. You can easily arrange your outing and choose from various launch points.

Guided Tours: If you're new to kayaking or paddleboarding, you may opt for guided tours that offer instruction, equipment, and a knowledgeable guide to ensure a safe and enjoyable experience.

Fitness and Relaxation: Paddling on the rivers is a great way to stay active while enjoying the outdoors. It's also a relaxing and peaceful activity, allowing you to unwind and connect with nature.

Nature Observation: You'll have the opportunity to observe wildlife, including birds, fish, and other creatures that call the rivers home. Keep an eye out for herons, ducks, and the occasional bald eagle.

Night Paddling: Some outfitters offer night paddling experiences, allowing you to enjoy the city's illuminated skyline and bridges from the water.

Family-Friendly: Kayaking and paddleboarding are family-friendly activities, suitable for people of various ages and skill levels.

Waterfront Dining: After your adventure, you can enjoy waterfront dining at various restaurants along the riverbanks, combining outdoor recreation with a delicious meal.

Seasonal Activities: Kayaking and paddleboarding are available seasonally, generally from spring to early autumn when the weather is pleasant and the rivers are accessible.

Before embarking on your kayaking or paddleboarding adventure, be sure to check with rental providers for equipment availability, launch locations, safety guidelines, and any specific rules or regulations for the rivers. It's a fantastic way to enjoy both the urban and natural aspects of Pittsburgh, creating a memorable and picturesque experience.

27.Discover the Children's Museum of Pittsburgh.

The Children's Museum of Pittsburgh is an engaging and interactive educational institution dedicated to providing children and families with creative and immersive learning experiences. Here's what you can expect when you discover the Children's Museum of Pittsburgh:

Interactive Exhibits: The museum features a wide array of interactive and hands-on exhibits designed to stimulate children's curiosity and encourage exploration. These exhibits cover various topics, from art and science to technology and culture.

Art Studio: Children can unleash their creativity in the museum's art studio, where they can experiment with various art materials and engage in artistic activities.

Water Play: The Waterplay exhibit allows kids to explore the properties of water, experiment with fluid dynamics, and enjoy water-based play in a controlled and safe environment.

Theater: The museum often hosts live performances, puppet shows, and theatrical productions that entertain and educate children through the magic of storytelling and drama.

Interactive Workshops: Educational workshops and programs are available to foster learning in subjects such as science, engineering, and the arts.

Gardens: The museum features an outdoor garden where children can experience nature, explore sensory play, and learn about gardening.

Makerspace: The MAKESHOP is a collaborative workspace where children can engage in hands-on making and building activities using various tools and materials.

Early Childhood Programs: The museum provides programs specifically designed for young children to promote early childhood development and learning through play.

Technology Integration: Technology-based exhibits and activities, including digital art and coding, are available to introduce children to the world of technology and innovation.

Community Engagement: The Children's Museum collaborates with the local community to bring in artists, educators, and experts to provide unique learning experiences.

Inclusive Environment: The museum is committed to providing an inclusive and welcoming environment for children of all abilities.

Educational Events: The museum hosts educational events, themed days, and special programming throughout the year, offering additional opportunities for fun and learning.

Café and Gift Shop: Enjoy a meal or snack at the museum's café, and explore the gift shop for unique educational toys and gifts.

The Children's Museum of Pittsburgh is a place of wonder, exploration, and creativity, offering children and families a safe and inspiring space to learn through play. It's a wonderful destination for fostering a love of learning, sparking imagination, and providing children with a rich and interactive educational experience.

28.Take a tour of Allegheny Cemetery.

Taking a tour of Allegheny Cemetery is a fascinating and historically rich experience. Located in Pittsburgh, Allegheny Cemetery is one of the oldest and largest cemeteries in the United States, and it's not just a place for reflection on the departed but also a testament to the city's history. Here's what you can expect when you explore Allegheny Cemetery:

Historical Significance: Established in 1844, Allegheny Cemetery has a rich history and is the final resting place for numerous notable individuals from Pittsburgh's past.

Architectural Beauty: The cemetery boasts stunning architectural elements, including ornate mausoleums, grand monuments, and beautifully landscaped gardens. The diverse styles of tombstones and memorials are a testament to the various time periods and architectural trends.

Landscaped Grounds: The cemetery covers a vast expanse of land, providing a peaceful and green sanctuary in the heart of the city. You can explore winding paths, open spaces, and tree-lined avenues.

Historical Figures: Allegheny Cemetery is the final resting place for many prominent Pittsburghers, including business tycoons, political leaders, writers, and military figures. You can find the graves of notable individuals like Stephen C. Foster, the composer of "Oh! Susanna," and renowned department store magnate Richard B. Mellon.

Art and Sculpture: The cemetery features a collection of impressive sculptures and artistry, contributing to the serene and contemplative atmosphere.

Guided Tours: The cemetery often offers guided tours that provide historical insights and stories about the notable figures buried there and the cemetery's architectural significance.

Genealogical Research: Allegheny Cemetery can be a valuable resource for genealogical research, and staff can assist visitors in locating graves and obtaining historical information.

Natural Beauty: The cemetery's landscape is home to a variety of trees, plants, and wildlife, making it a peaceful retreat for nature enthusiasts.

Community Events: The cemetery sometimes hosts community events, such as outdoor concerts, historical reenactments, and educational programs.

Tranquil Setting: It's a place for reflection and serenity, offering a quiet escape from the city's hustle and bustle.

Visiting Allegheny Cemetery offers a unique blend of history, architecture, art, and contemplation. It's an opportunity to explore Pittsburgh's past and pay respects to the individuals who have played a significant role in the city's development. Whether you're interested in history, architecture, or simply seeking a peaceful and beautiful setting, Allegheny Cemetery is a unique and culturally rich destination to explore.

29.Explore the historic Carrie Furnaces.

Exploring the historic Carrie Furnaces is a captivating journey back in time to the industrial heritage of Pittsburgh. The Carrie Furnaces, once part of the U.S. Steel Homestead Steel Works, offer a glimpse into the city's steelmaking past. Here's what you can expect when you explore the historic Carrie Furnaces:

Industrial Relics: The Carrie Furnaces are preserved blast furnaces that have been designated as a National Historic Landmark. They represent a significant piece of Pittsburgh's industrial history.

Guided Tours: The site is not open for self-guided tours. Instead, guided tours are available, typically led by knowledgeable guides who provide insights into the history and significance of the furnaces.

Steel Production History: During the tour, you'll learn about the steel production process and the crucial role that the furnaces played in the region's development.

Massive Structures: The blast furnaces are massive structures, towering over the landscape. You'll have the opportunity to explore the exterior of these towering giants.

Urban Decay and Art: The site's industrial decay and graffiti art create a striking juxtaposition, reflecting the transition of these structures from industrial powerhouses to symbols of urban decay.

Photography: The site is a popular spot for urban exploration and industrial photography due to its unique and visually striking aesthetic.

Educational Experience: The guided tours offer an educational experience, shedding light on the challenges and triumphs of the steel industry and the workers who played a crucial role in it.

Community Engagement: The site is a symbol of Pittsburgh's resilience and transformation from an industrial hub to a modern, diversified city.

Events and Workshops: The Carrie Furnaces occasionally host special events, workshops, and artistic projects, celebrating the site's historical and cultural significance.

Adjacent Sites: The furnaces are located in proximity to other historical and cultural sites, such as the Waterfront shopping district, offering additional attractions to explore in the area.

Visiting the historic Carrie Furnaces is a remarkable way to connect with Pittsburgh's industrial past and appreciate the city's evolution. It's a site of both historical significance and artistic expression, and the guided tours provide a unique opportunity to explore the legacy of steelmaking that has left an indelible mark on Pittsburgh's identity.

30. Attend a Pittsburgh Symphony Orchestra performance.

Attending a performance by the Pittsburgh Symphony Orchestra is a delightful and culturally enriching experience. As one of the premier orchestras in the United States, the Pittsburgh Symphony Orchestra offers world-class classical music and symphonic performances. Here's what you can expect when you attend a Pittsburgh Symphony Orchestra performance:

Classical Music Excellence: The Pittsburgh Symphony Orchestra is known for its exceptional musicianship and artistic quality. You can expect outstanding renditions of classical masterpieces, contemporary compositions, and orchestral works.

Historic Venue: Performances often take place at the historic Heinz Hall for the Performing Arts in downtown Pittsburgh, a beautifully restored venue that offers exceptional acoustics and a luxurious atmosphere.

Diverse Repertoire: The orchestra's repertoire spans a wide range of classical music, from the works of classical masters like Beethoven and Mozart to contemporary and innovative compositions.

Guest Soloists: The orchestra frequently collaborates with renowned guest soloists, including world-class pianists, violinists, cellists, and vocalists, adding depth and variety to their performances.

Pops Concerts: In addition to classical performances, the Pittsburgh Symphony Orchestra offers pops concerts that feature popular and film music, attracting a diverse audience.

Conductor Excellence: The orchestra is led by talented conductors who bring out the best in the musicians and ensure captivating and emotionally resonant performances.

Educational Initiatives: The Pittsburgh Symphony Orchestra is committed to education and community engagement. They offer educational programs, youth concerts, and opportunities for students to connect with classical music.

Holiday Performances: Seasonal performances, including holiday concerts, are a highlight of the orchestra's schedule, offering festive and heartwarming music for the community.

Post-Concert Events: Some performances may have post-concert events, such as meet-and-greets with musicians, to enhance the overall concert experience.

Cultural Experience: Attending a Pittsburgh Symphony Orchestra performance is a cultural experience that allows you to connect with the rich and timeless tradition of classical music.

Before attending a performance, be sure to check the orchestra's schedule, purchase tickets in advance, and consider any special themes or events associated with the concert. Whether you're a seasoned classical music enthusiast or a newcomer to the world of symphonic music, the Pittsburgh Symphony Orchestra offers a captivating and enriching cultural experience.

31.Visit the Clemente Museum, dedicated to baseball legend Roberto Clemente.

Visiting the Clemente Museum is a unique opportunity to learn about and pay tribute to one of baseball's greatest legends, Roberto Clemente. The museum is located in Pittsburgh and is dedicated to preserving the legacy of this iconic sports figure. Here's what you can expect when you visit the Clemente Museum:

Roberto Clemente's Legacy: The museum is a comprehensive showcase of Roberto Clemente's life, career, and contributions, both on and off the baseball field.

Exclusive Memorabilia: You'll have the chance to see an extensive collection of Clemente's personal memorabilia, including uniforms, awards, baseball equipment, and personal belongings.

Historical Context: The museum provides historical context on Clemente's impact on the sport of baseball, his humanitarian efforts, and his role as a pioneering figure for Latin American athletes.

Photographic Archives: There's a significant emphasis on photography, and you'll find a vast archive of images capturing Clemente's career and personal life.

Interactive Exhibits: The museum often incorporates interactive exhibits that engage visitors and help them connect with Clemente's experiences.

Community Outreach: Learn about Clemente's dedication to community service, his philanthropic efforts, and his commitment to helping those in need.

Educational Programs: The museum may offer educational programs, workshops, and special events, including lectures, to further explore the life and impact of Roberto Clemente.

Social and Cultural Significance: The museum highlights the broader social and cultural significance of Clemente's life, including his role as a Latino trailblazer in professional sports.

Gift Shop: You can browse the museum's gift shop for memorabilia, books, and souvenirs related to Roberto Clemente and baseball.

Inspiration: Visiting the Clemente Museum serves as an inspiring experience, showcasing the power of determination, compassion, and sportsmanship.

The Clemente Museum is a place where sports enthusiasts, history buffs, and those interested in the intersection of sports and culture can come together to honor the extraordinary life of a baseball legend and humanitarian. It's a must-visit for anyone seeking to gain a deeper understanding of the enduring legacy of Roberto Clemente.

32.Enjoy a picnic in Frick Park.

Frick Park is a beautiful and expansive urban park in Pittsburgh, Pennsylvania, offering a perfect setting for a relaxing picnic surrounded by nature. Here's what you can expect when you enjoy a picnic in Frick Park:

Natural Beauty: Frick Park is known for its lush greenery, woodlands, and meadows, providing a picturesque backdrop for your picnic.

Trails: The park features an extensive network of hiking and walking trails, allowing you to explore the natural landscape before or after your picnic.

Picnic Areas: There are designated picnic areas equipped with tables, benches, and grills, making it easy to set up your picnic and enjoy a meal outdoors.

Shelter Rentals: If you plan a larger gathering or want shelter from the elements, you can rent picnic shelters for group picnics and events.

Wildlife: Frick Park is home to a variety of wildlife, and you might spot birds, squirrels, and other animals as you dine.

Playgrounds: If you have children with you, the park offers playgrounds where they can enjoy some playtime before or after your picnic.

Educational Opportunities: The park often hosts educational programs and events, allowing visitors to learn more about the natural environment and conservation efforts.

Sports and Recreation: Frick Park provides opportunities for sports and recreational activities, including tennis, baseball, and more. You can work off your picnic meal with some physical activity.

Cultural and Artistic Features: The park occasionally hosts cultural events, outdoor concerts, and artistic installations.

Peaceful Atmosphere: Frick Park's serene environment makes it an ideal spot for relaxation, meditation, or a leisurely stroll.

Dog-Friendly: The park is dog-friendly, and you can bring your canine companions along for a picnic and a walk. There's also a designated off-leash area for dogs to play.

Year-Round Enjoyment: Frick Park offers something to enjoy in every season, whether it's a spring picnic, summer hiking, colorful autumn foliage, or a winter walk in the snow.

Remember to pack a picnic basket with your favorite foods and drinks, and perhaps a blanket to sit on. Be sure to follow park rules and clean up after your picnic to help preserve the beauty of Frick Park for future visitors. Enjoy your time in this peaceful urban oasis.

33. Take a ride on the Monongahela Incline.

Taking a ride on the Monongahela Incline is a classic and iconic Pittsburgh experience. The Monongahela Incline is one of the city's historic funicular railways, providing breathtaking views and a fun way to access the Mount Washington neighborhood. Here's what you can expect when you ride the Monongahela Incline:

Historic Transportation: The Monongahela Incline, originally built in 1870, is one of Pittsburgh's two remaining funiculars and is listed on the National Register of Historic Places.

Scenic Views: As the incline ascends or descends Mount Washington, you'll be treated to stunning panoramic views of downtown Pittsburgh, the three rivers (Allegheny, Monongahela, and Ohio), and the city's skyline.

Unique Perspective: Riding the incline offers a unique and memorable way to see Pittsburgh from a vantage point that is different from any other. It's especially spectacular at night when the city's lights twinkle.

Short Ride: The incline ride is relatively short, taking just a few minutes, but it provides an opportunity for fantastic photos and a scenic experience.

Funicular Operation: The incline operates with a counterbalance system, and as one car ascends, the other descends, providing a safe and smooth ride.

Mount Washington: At the top of the incline, you'll arrive at Grandview Avenue on Mount Washington, known for its overlooks, restaurants, and a scenic promenade.

Dining and Shopping: Once you reach Mount Washington, you can explore the various dining and shopping options along Grandview Avenue, making it a great place to relax and enjoy a meal or a souvenir.

Photography: The Monongahela Incline and its surroundings offer excellent photo opportunities, capturing the beauty of Pittsburgh and its iconic landmarks.

Historical Plaque: At the upper station, you can find a historical plaque that provides information about the incline's history and significance.

Return Trip: When you're ready to return, simply hop back on the incline for the descent back to the station near the riverbanks.

Riding the Monongahela Incline is a quintessential Pittsburgh experience, allowing you to appreciate the city's topography and take in its breathtaking views. It's a favorite activity for tourists and locals alike, and it offers a unique and memorable perspective on the Steel City.

34.Explore Bicycle Heaven, the world's largest bicycle museum.

Bicycle Heaven is a fascinating and unique attraction located in Pittsburgh, Pennsylvania, known as the world's largest bicycle museum and shop. Here's what you can expect when you explore Bicycle Heaven:

Extensive Collection: Bicycle Heaven boasts a vast and eclectic collection of bicycles, including vintage, rare, and historic models. You can expect to see bicycles from various eras and styles.

Historical Insights: The museum provides historical context and information about the evolution of bicycles, from early designs to modern innovations.

Interactive Displays: Many exhibits are interactive, allowing visitors to get up close to the bicycles and even try some of them out.

Bicycle Art: In addition to the functional bicycles, the museum features bicycle-related artwork and decorative pieces, showcasing the artistic and creative side of bike culture.

Accessories and Memorabilia: Bicycle Heaven is not just about bicycles; it also includes a wide range of cycling accessories, memorabilia, and ephemera, providing a complete picture of cycling culture.

Bike Restoration: The museum often showcases the process of bicycle restoration, offering insights into the effort and care that goes into preserving vintage and historic bikes.

Cycling History: Learn about the role of bicycles in transportation, recreation, and culture, and how they have impacted society over the years.

Retail Shop: Bicycle Heaven includes a retail shop where you can purchase vintage and retro bicycle parts, accessories, and collectibles.

Cycling Enthusiast Destination: It's a must-visit for cycling enthusiasts, collectors, and anyone interested in the history of bicycles and their cultural significance.

Family-Friendly: The museum is family-friendly, making it a great place for kids and adults alike to explore and learn together.

Bicycle Heaven is more than just a museum; it's a celebration of the bicycle's cultural and historical significance. It provides an opportunity to step back in time and appreciate the evolution of cycling while also enjoying the creative and artistic aspects of bicycle culture. Whether you're a dedicated cyclist or simply curious about the world of bikes, this museum offers a unique and informative experience.

35. Visit the Western Pennsylvania Model Railroad Museum.

The Western Pennsylvania Model Railroad Museum is a delightful destination for model railroad enthusiasts and anyone with an interest in trains. Located in Pittsburgh, Pennsylvania, the museum showcases intricate miniature landscapes and model train layouts. Here's what you can expect when you visit the Western Pennsylvania Model Railroad Museum:

Intricate Model Railroads: The museum features an extensive collection of model train layouts, ranging from large and detailed displays to smaller dioramas. You can explore miniature worlds with realistic landscapes, towns, and train systems.

Educational Experience: The museum offers educational exhibits and information about the history of railroads in Western Pennsylvania, providing insights into the region's rich railroad heritage.

Interactive Displays: Some areas of the museum offer interactive elements, allowing visitors, especially children, to control trains and operate various parts of the model railroads.

Seasonal Displays: The museum often features seasonal displays that celebrate holidays like Christmas, with themed trains and festive decorations.

Historical Accuracy: Attention to detail is a hallmark of the museum, with an emphasis on historical accuracy in recreating train operations, landscapes, and architecture.

Scale Models: Different scales and types of model trains are on display, showcasing the variety within the world of model railroading.

Special Events: The museum hosts special events, workshops, and model train-related activities, attracting model railroading enthusiasts and families alike.

Gift Shop: You can browse the museum's gift shop for model train-related merchandise, including model train sets, accessories, and railroad memorabilia.

Community and Social: The museum often acts as a hub for the local model railroading community, fostering a sense of camaraderie among enthusiasts.

Family-Friendly: The museum is family-friendly, making it an enjoyable experience for visitors of all ages.

Visiting the Western Pennsylvania Model Railroad Museum is like stepping into a world of miniature railways and landscapes, where creativity, attention to detail, and a love of trains come to life. Whether you're a lifelong model railroad enthusiast or simply curious about this fascinating hobby, the museum provides a captivating and educational experience that's sure to delight.

36.Explore the Roberto Clemente Bridge.

Exploring the Roberto Clemente Bridge in Pittsburgh is a wonderful way to take in the city's iconic architecture, enjoy scenic views, and immerse yourself in the vibrant atmosphere of downtown Pittsburgh. Here's what you can expect when you explore the Roberto Clemente Bridge:

Historical Significance: The Roberto Clemente Bridge, formerly known as the Sixth Street Bridge, is named in honor of the legendary baseball player Roberto Clemente. It's a tribute to his contributions on and off the field.

Stunning Views: The bridge spans the Allegheny River and offers stunning panoramic views of Pittsburgh's skyline, particularly during sunrise and sunset. It's a popular spot for photographers and sightseers.

Cultural District: The bridge connects the downtown area with the city's Cultural District, which is home to theaters, art galleries, restaurants, and entertainment venues. It's a lively and cultural hub.

Bridge Festivals: At certain times of the year, the bridge is closed to vehicular traffic to host special events and festivals. These events often feature live music, food vendors, and a festive atmosphere.

Walkability: The bridge is pedestrian-friendly, with dedicated walkways for strolling, jogging, and taking leisurely walks. It's a favorite spot for locals and visitors to enjoy a scenic walk.

Biking: Bicyclists can also use the bridge's dedicated bike lanes to cross the river and explore the city.

Public Art: Along the bridge, you'll find various public art installations and sculptures that contribute to the city's vibrant art scene.

Night Illumination: The Roberto Clemente Bridge is beautifully illuminated at night, adding to its charm and making it an attractive spot for an evening walk.

Nearby Attractions: In addition to the Cultural District, the bridge is within walking distance of other Pittsburgh attractions, including PNC Park, the Andy Warhol Museum, and the Carnegie Science Center.

Clemente Statue: At the northern end of the bridge, near PNC Park, there's a statue of Roberto Clemente that serves as a lasting tribute to the baseball legend.

Exploring the Roberto Clemente Bridge is a fantastic way to appreciate Pittsburgh's urban beauty, immerse yourself in its cultural offerings, and enjoy picturesque views of the city. Whether you're taking a leisurely walk, capturing the cityscape with your camera, or simply enjoying the ambiance of downtown Pittsburgh, the bridge offers a memorable and authentic Pittsburgh experience.

37.Attend a live theater performance at City Theatre.

Attending a live theater performance at City Theatre in Pittsburgh is an immersive and culturally enriching experience. City Theatre is a renowned venue for contemporary and innovative theater productions. Here's what you can expect when you attend a show at City Theatre:

Contemporary Productions: City Theatre is known for its commitment to producing contemporary and cutting-edge theatrical works, including world premieres of new plays.

Intimate Setting: The theater provides an intimate and cozy atmosphere, allowing for a more personal and engaging connection with the performances.

Diverse Programming: City Theatre offers a diverse range of programming, from thought-provoking dramas and comedies to musicals and experimental theater.

Talented Cast and Crew: The theater features talented actors, directors, and designers who bring compelling and thought-provoking stories to life.

Community Engagement: City Theatre often engages with the community through post-show discussions, talkbacks, and educational outreach programs to enhance the audience's understanding and appreciation of the performances.

Flexible Seating: The theater provides flexible seating options, allowing for various seating configurations to suit the specific needs of each production.

Access to New Works: Many productions at City Theatre are world premieres or regional premieres, giving the audience a chance to experience new and groundbreaking works.

Themed Seasons: The theater often organizes its productions around themed seasons, offering a cohesive and thoughtfully curated theatrical experience.

Cultural Relevance: City Theatre's productions often touch on relevant social and cultural themes, sparking conversations and reflection.

Café and Lounge: The theater includes a café and lounge where you can enjoy refreshments and mingle with other theatergoers before or after the show.

Before attending a performance at City Theatre, be sure to check the schedule for the current production lineup, purchase tickets in advance, and explore any special events or extras associated with the shows. Whether you're a theater enthusiast or a first-time theatergoer, City Theatre provides a unique and artistic experience that celebrates the vibrant world of contemporary theater.

38.Take a walk in Highland Park and see the Pittsburgh Reservoir.

Highland Park is a beautiful and expansive urban park in Pittsburgh, Pennsylvania, offering a serene natural retreat within the city. When you take a walk in Highland Park, you'll have the opportunity to enjoy the picturesque landscapes and visit the Pittsburgh Reservoir. Here's what you can expect during your visit:

Natural Beauty: Highland Park is known for its lush greenery, mature trees, and well-maintained landscapes, providing a peaceful and scenic environment for your walk.

Reservoir: The Pittsburgh Reservoir, also known as the Highland Park Reservoir, is a picturesque body of water located within the park. It serves as a reservoir for the city's drinking water supply.

Walking Paths: The park offers a network of walking paths and trails, allowing you to explore the reservoir and its surroundings on foot. The paths wind through the park and provide a great opportunity for a leisurely stroll.

Peaceful Setting: The reservoir area is often less crowded than other parts of the park, creating a tranquil and reflective atmosphere for your walk.

Bridges: Several charming bridges span the reservoir, offering lovely views and photo opportunities. The bridges add to the park's aesthetic appeal.

Wildlife: Highland Park is home to a variety of wildlife, including ducks, geese, and other birds that frequent the reservoir. It's a great place for birdwatching and nature observation.

Picnic Areas: The park features designated picnic areas if you want to enjoy a meal in a scenic outdoor setting.

Botanical Garden: Adjacent to the park, you'll find the Pittsburgh Zoo & PPG Aquarium and the Phipps Conservatory and Botanical Gardens, which are wonderful attractions to explore in the vicinity.

Seasonal Beauty: The park offers a different kind of beauty in each season, from the vibrant colors of spring and summer to the stunning fall foliage and even the peaceful tranquility of winter.

Relaxation: Whether you're looking for a peaceful retreat, a spot for meditation, or simply a lovely place for a casual walk, Highland Park and the reservoir provide a welcoming environment.

Taking a walk in Highland Park and visiting the Pittsburgh Reservoir allows you to connect with nature, escape the hustle and bustle of the city, and appreciate the scenic and natural beauty that Pittsburgh has to offer. It's an ideal spot for relaxation, recreation, and enjoying the outdoors.

39.Discover the August Wilson House, the childhood home of the playwright.

The August Wilson House is a significant cultural and historical site located in Pittsburgh, Pennsylvania, and it's the childhood home of the renowned playwright August Wilson. Here's what you can expect when you visit the August Wilson House:

Historical Significance: The house is the childhood home of August Wilson, an iconic African American playwright celebrated for his powerful and influential works, including "Fences," "The Piano Lesson," and "Ma Rainey's Black Bottom."

Museum and Cultural Center: The August Wilson House is now a museum and cultural center dedicated to preserving and celebrating the life and work of August Wilson.

Exhibits: The house features exhibits that showcase the life and career of August Wilson, his contributions to American theater, and his cultural impact.

Community Engagement: The cultural center often hosts community events, educational programs, workshops, and artistic performances, fostering an appreciation for the arts and African American culture.

Guided Tours: Visitors can take guided tours of the house, which provide historical insights into August Wilson's upbringing, early influences, and the places that inspired his literary creations.

Archival Materials: The museum includes a collection of archival materials, manuscripts, and personal items related to August Wilson's life and writing.

Historical Preservation: The August Wilson House is a testament to the preservation of African American history and culture in Pittsburgh, with an emphasis on the Hill District, a neighborhood rich in African American heritage.

Educational Initiatives: The cultural center often collaborates with schools and educational institutions to promote literacy, the arts, and African American history.

Artistic Performances: The center occasionally hosts artistic performances and events inspired by August Wilson's works, providing a platform for cultural expression.

Community Impact: The August Wilson House serves as a hub for community engagement and a source of inspiration, fostering dialogue, creativity, and appreciation for the arts.

Visiting the August Wilson House is an opportunity to delve into the life and legacy of a Pulitzer Prize-winning playwright and to learn about the cultural and artistic contributions of African Americans in the United States. It's a place to gain insights into the history and cultural vibrancy of Pittsburgh's Hill District and celebrate a literary icon whose work continues to resonate with audiences worldwide.

40.Enjoy a jazz performance at the Manchester Craftsmen's Guild.

Experiencing a jazz performance at the Manchester Craftsmen's Guild in Pittsburgh is a captivating and culturally enriching experience. The guild is known for its commitment to the arts and music, particularly jazz. Here's what you can expect when you attend a jazz performance at the Manchester Craftsmen's Guild:

Jazz Excellence: The Manchester Craftsmen's Guild is renowned for its exceptional jazz performances, featuring both established and emerging jazz musicians and ensembles.

Intimate Setting: The venue provides an intimate and acoustically superb setting, allowing for a closer connection with the musicians and a more immersive jazz experience.

Diverse Programming: The guild offers a diverse range of jazz programming, including traditional, contemporary, and experimental jazz styles. You can expect to enjoy a wide spectrum of jazz music.

Talented Musicians: Performances often feature world-class jazz musicians, showcasing their virtuosity and improvisational skills.

Educational Initiatives: The Manchester Craftsmen's Guild is dedicated to arts education and offers various programs, including jazz education and workshops for students and aspiring musicians.

Artistic Expression: Jazz performances at the guild reflect the artistic expression and creativity that are central to the jazz genre.

Community Engagement: The guild fosters community engagement and often collaborates with schools, community organizations, and local artists to promote jazz appreciation and education.

Café and Lounge: The venue often includes a café or lounge area where you can enjoy refreshments, mingle with fellow jazz enthusiasts, and discuss the performances.

Special Events: The guild hosts special events, jazz festivals, and thematic jazz programs throughout the year.

Cultural Enrichment: Attending a jazz performance at the Manchester Craftsmen's Guild provides a unique and culturally enriching experience, celebrating the rich heritage of jazz music.

Before attending a performance, be sure to check the schedule for the current jazz lineup, purchase tickets in advance, and explore any special events or educational opportunities associated with the shows. Whether you're a dedicated jazz aficionado or a newcomer to the world of jazz, the Manchester Craftsmen's Guild offers an intimate and immersive jazz experience that celebrates the artistry and improvisational spirit of this influential musical genre.

41.Take a bike ride on the Great Allegheny Passage trail.

Taking a bike ride on the Great Allegheny Passage (GAP) trail is a fantastic way to experience the natural beauty and cultural heritage of the region. The GAP is a scenic rail-trail that spans from Pittsburgh, Pennsylvania, to Cumberland, Maryland, and connects with the C&O Canal Towpath, ultimately reaching Washington, D.C. Here's what you can expect when you embark on a bike ride on the Great Allegheny Passage trail:

Scenic Beauty: The GAP trail offers breathtaking views of the Allegheny Mountains, river valleys, and charming towns along the way. You'll be surrounded by natural beauty throughout your ride.

Historic Rail-Trail: The trail follows the former route of the Western Maryland Railway and features several historic sites and structures, including old train stations and tunnels.

Variety of Terrain: The trail offers a variety of terrain, from flat and easy sections to challenging inclines and descents. Cyclists of all skill levels can enjoy the ride.

Tunnels and Bridges: The GAP includes several tunnels and bridges, adding to the adventure and providing a unique cycling experience.

Biking Amenities: The trail is well-maintained, with bike-friendly amenities such as rest areas, water stations, and campsites along the way.

Cultural Attractions: You'll pass through or near towns that have museums, historical sites, and cultural attractions, offering opportunities to explore the local heritage.

Wildlife and Nature: The trail provides a chance to observe wildlife, birds, and diverse plant life as you cycle through natural areas and parklands.

Overnight Stops: The trail offers places to camp or stay in small towns along the route, making it possible to take a multi-day bike trip.

Local Dining: You'll have the opportunity to sample local cuisine and enjoy dining in the towns and communities you pass through.

Connection to C&O Canal Towpath: The Great Allegheny Passage seamlessly connects to the C&O Canal Towpath in Cumberland, Maryland, offering a long-distance biking experience to Washington, D.C.

Before setting out on your bike ride, it's a good idea to plan your route, check trail conditions, and ensure you have the appropriate gear, including a well-maintained bicycle. Whether you're a dedicated cyclist looking for an extended journey or a casual rider seeking a scenic day trip, the Great Allegheny Passage trail offers a memorable and diverse cycling adventure with breathtaking views and a connection to the region's history and culture.

42. Attend a Pittsburgh Ballet Theatre performance.

Attending a Pittsburgh Ballet Theatre (PBT) performance is a delightful and culturally enriching experience. PBT is a renowned ballet company in Pittsburgh, Pennsylvania, known for its exceptional dancers and captivating productions. Here's what you can expect when you attend a ballet performance by the Pittsburgh Ballet Theatre:

World-Class Ballet: PBT is known for its world-class ballet performances, showcasing the artistry, grace, and talent of its dancers. The company often stages classic ballets, contemporary works, and innovative productions.

Beautiful Venues: Performances typically take place in some of Pittsburgh's beautiful and historic venues, such as the Benedum Center for the Performing Arts, where you can enjoy excellent acoustics and a stunning atmosphere.

Variety of Repertoire: PBT offers a diverse repertoire, including timeless classics like "Swan Lake" and "The Nutcracker," as well as modern works that push the boundaries of ballet.

Talented Dancers: The company's performances feature exceptionally skilled and expressive ballet dancers who bring the choreography to life.

Choreographic Excellence: PBT often collaborates with renowned choreographers to create innovative and dynamic productions that captivate audiences.

Educational Initiatives: The ballet company is dedicated to education and community outreach, offering programs for students and the community to learn about and engage with ballet.

Guest Artists: You may have the opportunity to see guest artists from around the world who occasionally perform with PBT, adding an extra layer of artistry to the productions.

Cultural Enrichment: Attending a PBT performance allows you to immerse yourself in the world of classical and contemporary ballet, appreciating the skill and artistry of the dancers and choreographers.

Storytelling: Ballet productions often tell beautiful and emotional stories, conveying narratives through movement and dance.

Elegant Atmosphere: Attending a ballet performance is a chance to dress up, enjoy an elegant night out, and experience the timeless charm of ballet.

Before attending a performance, be sure to check PBT's schedule, purchase tickets in advance, and explore any special events or educational programs associated with the show. Whether you're a dedicated ballet enthusiast or someone looking to explore the world of dance, the Pittsburgh Ballet Theatre offers a captivating and memorable artistic experience that celebrates the beauty of ballet.

43.Explore the Beechview-Seldom Seen Greenway.

The Beechview-Seldom Seen Greenway is a delightful outdoor destination in Pittsburgh, Pennsylvania, providing a serene and natural escape for visitors. Here's what you can expect when you explore the Beechview-Seldom Seen Greenway:

Natural Beauty: The greenway offers a peaceful and scenic environment, with lush greenery, native plants, and natural landscapes providing a refreshing escape from the urban environment.

Trails: The greenway features walking and hiking trails that wind through the natural surroundings, making it a great spot for leisurely walks, jogging, and enjoying the outdoors.

Historic Viaduct: The greenway is home to the Beechview-Seldom Seen Viaduct, a historic railroad bridge that has been repurposed for pedestrian and recreational use. The viaduct offers elevated views and is a unique feature of the greenway.

Birdwatching: The greenway's natural habitat attracts a variety of bird species, making it an excellent place for birdwatching and nature observation.

Community Garden: You might come across community gardens and green spaces along the greenway, where local residents cultivate plants and vegetables.

Picnic Areas: There are designated picnic areas and rest spots where you can enjoy a meal, relax, or take in the scenery.

Local Art: The greenway sometimes features local art installations, sculptures, and creative projects that add to the natural and artistic ambiance.

Wildlife: In addition to birdwatching, the greenway is a habitat for various wildlife, such as squirrels and other small animals.

Family-Friendly: The greenway provides a family-friendly environment, making it a wonderful place for parents and children to explore and enjoy together.

Peaceful Atmosphere: Whether you're seeking a place for relaxation, meditation, or simply a peaceful stroll, the Beechview-Seldom Seen Greenway offers a tranquil atmosphere.

Before visiting the greenway, you may want to check for any events or guided tours that could enhance your experience. Whether you're a nature enthusiast, a local resident, or a visitor to Pittsburgh, the Beechview-Seldom Seen Greenway is an inviting and natural oasis within the city, offering an opportunity to connect with the outdoors and appreciate the beauty of the region.

44. Visit the Pittsburgh Glass Center.

Visiting the Pittsburgh Glass Center is a captivating and creative experience that allows you to explore the art and craft of glassmaking. Located in Pittsburgh, Pennsylvania, the center serves as a hub for glass artists and enthusiasts. Here's what you can expect when you visit the Pittsburgh Glass Center:

Glass Art: The center is home to a stunning collection of glass art, including sculptures, vessels, and various glasswork created by local and international artists.

Glassblowing Demonstrations: Visitors have the opportunity to witness live glassblowing demonstrations by skilled artists, where molten glass is transformed into intricate shapes and forms.

Glass Workshops: The Pittsburgh Glass Center offers a range of workshops for all skill levels, allowing you to try your hand at glassblowing, kiln-forming, flameworking, and more.

Resident Artists: The center often hosts resident artists who work on-site, and you can interact with them and gain insights into their creative process.

Exhibitions: The center regularly hosts glass art exhibitions, showcasing the works of emerging and established glass artists.

Glass Sales: You can purchase unique glass art pieces, ornaments, and functional glassware in the center's shop, offering a selection of beautiful and handmade items.

Community Engagement: The Pittsburgh Glass Center is deeply involved in the community and offers outreach programs, glass art classes for youth, and educational initiatives.

Studio Tours: Guided tours of the studio and facility provide a behind-the-scenes look at the glassmaking process and the equipment used by artists.

Glass Garden: The center's outdoor glass garden features stunning glass sculptures and installations set within a natural garden setting.

Event Space: The Pittsburgh Glass Center often hosts events, including glass art auctions, glass-making parties, and gatherings that celebrate glass art.

Before your visit, it's a good idea to check the center's schedule for workshops, demonstrations, and special events. Whether you're an aspiring glass artist, a fan of glass art, or simply curious about the art of glassblowing, a visit to the Pittsburgh Glass Center offers an engaging and creative experience that celebrates the beauty and craftsmanship of glass.

45.Experience the beauty of Raccoon Creek State Park (near Pittsburgh).

Raccoon Creek State Park, located near Pittsburgh, Pennsylvania, is a picturesque natural oasis that offers a wide range of outdoor activities and a chance to experience the beauty of the region. Here's what you can expect when you visit Raccoon Creek State Park:

Travel to Pittsburgh Pennsylvania

Scenic Landscapes: The park is known for its stunning natural beauty, including wooded areas, rolling hills, and the serene Raccoon Lake, which offers plenty of opportunities for photography and relaxation.

Hiking: Raccoon Creek State Park boasts numerous hiking trails that cater to various skill levels. You can explore the park's diverse ecosystems, enjoy the changing foliage, and even hike along the lakeshore.

Camping: The park offers a campground with both tent and RV sites, allowing you to immerse yourself in the great outdoors. Camping under the stars and next to the lake is a serene experience.

Fishing: Raccoon Lake is a popular spot for fishing, and you can expect to catch a variety of fish species, including bass, catfish, and trout. Fishing is permitted both from boats and the shoreline.

Boating: The lake is open to boating, making it an excellent spot for kayaking, canoeing, paddleboarding, and sailing. There's also a marina with boat rentals available.

Picnicking: The park offers picnic areas equipped with tables, grills, and scenic lake views. It's an ideal place for a family picnic or a leisurely lunch.

Swimming: Raccoon Creek State Park has a designated swimming area with a sandy beach. On a hot summer day, you can cool off in the refreshing waters of Raccoon Lake.

Birdwatching: The park's diverse habitats make it an excellent location for birdwatching. You may spot a variety of bird species, including waterfowl and migratory birds.

Wildlife Observation: Beyond birds, the park is home to diverse wildlife, such as deer, raccoons, and various aquatic creatures. It's a great place for nature enthusiasts.

Educational Programs: The park offers environmental education programs and events, providing opportunities for learning about the natural world and conservation.

Seasonal Activities: Raccoon Creek State Park offers different experiences in each season, from winter activities like cross-country skiing to the vibrant foliage of fall.

Photography: The park's landscapes and the changing seasons provide ample opportunities for photography and capturing the beauty of the outdoors.

Before your visit, consider checking the park's website for any special events or programs that may be occurring during your stay. Raccoon Creek State Park offers a diverse range of activities, ensuring that visitors of all interests can appreciate the natural beauty and recreational opportunities that the park has to offer.

46.Attend a Pittsburgh Opera performance.

Attending a Pittsburgh Opera performance is a cultural and artistic experience that allows you to immerse yourself in the world of opera and enjoy exceptional vocal performances. Here's what you can expect when you attend a Pittsburgh Opera performance:

Operatic Excellence: Pittsburgh Opera is known for its high-quality opera productions, featuring accomplished singers, musicians, and production teams.

Variety of Productions: The company stages a diverse repertoire of operas, from timeless classics like "La Traviata" and "Carmen" to contemporary works and lesser-known gems.

Beautiful Venues: Performances often take place in Pittsburgh's magnificent theaters, providing an elegant and acoustically superb setting for opera.

Talented Singers: Pittsburgh Opera showcases accomplished opera singers who bring emotional depth and artistry to their roles, delivering powerful and moving performances.

Orchestra and Chorus: Each production is accompanied by a talented orchestra and chorus, enriching the musical experience.

Stagecraft and Sets: The company's productions feature impressive sets, costumes, and stagecraft that transport audiences to the world of the opera's story.

Educational Initiatives: Pittsburgh Opera is dedicated to arts education and community engagement, offering programs and events that introduce opera to diverse audiences.

Pre-Performance Talks: Before some performances, the company provides pre-show talks that offer insights into the opera, its history, and the creative process.

Cultural Enrichment: Attending a Pittsburgh Opera performance allows you to immerse yourself in the world of opera, appreciate the vocal and dramatic artistry of the performers, and engage with the timeless stories.

Elegant Atmosphere: Going to an opera performance is an opportunity to dress up and enjoy a night out in a sophisticated and cultured environment.

Before attending a performance, be sure to check Pittsburgh Opera's schedule for the current season, purchase tickets in advance, and explore any special events or educational programs associated with the opera. Whether you're an opera enthusiast or someone looking to explore the world of vocal and theatrical art, Pittsburgh Opera offers a memorable and enriching artistic experience that celebrates the beauty and drama of opera.

47. Visit the Bicycle Museum of America.

The Bicycle Museum of America, located in New Bremen, Ohio, is a fascinating destination for bicycle enthusiasts and those interested in the history of cycling. Here's what you can expect when you visit the Bicycle Museum of America:

Historical Bicycle Collection: The museum houses an extensive collection of bicycles that span the history of cycling. You can explore a wide range of bicycles, from antique and vintage models to modern and innovative designs.

Evolution of Bicycle Technology: The museum provides insights into the evolution of bicycle technology, showcasing how bicycles have changed over the years in terms of design, materials, and functionality.

Rare and Unique Bicycles: You'll have the opportunity to see rare and unique bicycles, including early high-wheelers, safety bicycles, tandem bikes, and iconic models from different eras.

Artifacts and Memorabilia: In addition to bicycles, the museum displays various cycling-related artifacts, memorabilia, and historical documents that provide context to the history of cycling.

Educational Exhibits: The museum often features educational exhibits that explore the cultural, social, and technological impact of bicycles.

Bicycle Accessories: You can see a range of bicycle accessories, such as lights, bells, baskets, and gear, that were used with different types of bicycles.

Interactive Displays: Some sections of the museum may have interactive displays, allowing visitors to learn more about the mechanics and engineering behind bicycles.

Temporary Exhibitions: The museum hosts temporary exhibitions that focus on specific aspects of bicycle history, famous cyclists, or significant milestones in the world of cycling.

Community Engagement: The Bicycle Museum of America is engaged in the local community, offering educational programs, workshops, and events related to cycling and history.

Gift Shop: The museum typically has a gift shop where you can purchase bicycle-themed merchandise, souvenirs, and books related to cycling history.

Before planning your visit, it's a good idea to check the museum's website for current exhibitions, opening hours, and any special events or programs that may be taking place during your visit. Whether you're a passionate cyclist, a history buff, or simply curious about the evolution of transportation, the Bicycle Museum of America provides a unique and informative journey through the world of cycling history.

48.Explore the Johnny Angel's Ginchy Stuff and Music Museum.

Johnny Angel's Ginchy Stuff and Music Museum is a unique and quirky destination in Pittsburgh, Pennsylvania, offering a fascinating collection of pop culture and music memorabilia. Here's what you can expect when you explore Johnny Angel's Ginchy Stuff and Music Museum:

Eclectic Collection: The museum is known for its eclectic and extensive collection of music memorabilia, vintage toys, pop culture artifacts, and other "ginchy" items. It's a treasure trove of nostalgia.

Music History: The museum pays tribute to the history of music, with a particular focus on rock and roll, doo-wop, and other music genres. You can expect to see vintage records, instruments, concert posters, and more.

Vintage Toys: In addition to music memorabilia, the museum features a wide array of vintage toys, including action figures, board games, and collectibles that harken back to different eras.

Film and Television: Johnny Angel's collection often includes items related to classic films, television shows, and celebrities. You may encounter props, posters, and autographed items.

Cultural Artifacts: The museum showcases cultural artifacts that provide insights into the popular culture of bygone decades, offering a window into the past.

Elvis Room: One of the highlights is the "Elvis Room," dedicated to the King of Rock and Roll, Elvis Presley. It features a vast collection of Elvis memorabilia.

Music Performances: The museum occasionally hosts live music performances, special events, and themed exhibitions, creating a dynamic and engaging atmosphere.

Gift Shop: You'll typically find a gift shop where you can purchase music-related items, memorabilia, and souvenirs to take home.

Interactive Exhibits: Some sections of the museum may feature interactive exhibits or areas where you can listen to music and relive the sounds of the past.

Community Engagement: Johnny Angel's Ginchy Stuff and Music Museum is often involved in the local community, hosting events and contributing to the cultural scene in Pittsburgh.

Before your visit, it's a good idea to check the museum's website or social media channels for current exhibitions, opening hours, and any special events or performances that may be taking place during your visit. Whether you're a music enthusiast, a pop culture aficionado, or someone looking for a nostalgic journey through the past, Johnny Angel's Ginchy Stuff and Music Museum offers a unique and entertaining experience filled with an array of "ginchy" treasures.

49.Attend a comedy show at the Arcade Comedy Theater.

Attending a comedy show at the Arcade Comedy Theater in Pittsburgh is a night of laughter and entertainment. The theater is known for its improvisational and sketch comedy performances, as well as stand-up comedy. Here's what you can expect when you attend a comedy show at the Arcade Comedy Theater:

Comedic Excellence: The theater features talented comedians, improvisers, and sketch performers who are known for their wit and humor.

Improvisational Comedy: Many performances are based on audience suggestions and participation, creating an interactive and unpredictable comedy experience.

Sketch Comedy: You can expect to see well-crafted and hilarious sketch comedy routines that cover a range of topics and scenarios.

Stand-Up Comedy: The theater hosts stand-up comedy nights where you can enjoy the comedic stylings of local and touring stand-up comedians.

Varied Shows: The theater offers a diverse lineup of comedy shows, ensuring there's something for everyone, from family-friendly comedy to edgier, late-night humor.

Intimate Setting: The theater provides an intimate and cozy atmosphere, allowing for a more personal and immersive comedy experience.

Cultural Relevance: Comedy performances often touch on current events and social issues, providing a humorous perspective on contemporary culture.

Community Engagement: Arcade Comedy Theater is actively involved in the local comedy community, offering workshops, classes, and opportunities for emerging comedians to hone their craft.

Late-Night Shows: Some performances are scheduled for late-night entertainment, making it an ideal choice for those looking to end the evening with laughter.

Café and Lounge: The theater often includes a café or lounge area where you can enjoy refreshments and mingle with fellow comedy enthusiasts before or after the show.

Before attending a comedy show, be sure to check the Arcade Comedy Theater's schedule for the current lineup, purchase tickets in advance, and explore any special events or workshops associated with the performances. Whether you're a comedy aficionado or someone looking for a fun night out, the Arcade Comedy Theater provides a lively and entertaining experience filled with laughter and comedic talent.

50. Take a scenic drive through Ohiopyle State Park (near Pittsburgh).

A scenic drive through Ohiopyle State Park, located near Pittsburgh, Pennsylvania, is a picturesque journey through nature and offers breathtaking views of waterfalls, the Youghiogheny River, and lush forests. Here's what you can expect when you embark on a scenic drive through Ohiopyle State Park:

Natural Beauty: Ohiopyle State Park is known for its stunning natural beauty, with scenic overlooks and peaceful landscapes that are perfect for relaxation and exploration.

Ohiopyle Falls: The drive typically includes a stop at Ohiopyle Falls, a picturesque waterfall on the Youghiogheny River. You can take in the view from the observation area.

Youghiogheny River Gorge: The drive follows the Youghiogheny River Gorge, offering captivating views of the river, which is popular for white-water rafting and kayaking.

Lush Forests: The park is home to dense forests, providing opportunities for birdwatching and enjoying the changing foliage in different seasons.

Meadow Run Natural Waterslides: You may pass by the Meadow Run Natural Waterslides, a unique rock formation where visitors can slide down the naturally formed chutes.

Hiking Trails: The park features various hiking trails, so you can choose to explore the natural beauty on foot if you prefer.

Picnic Areas: Scenic pull-offs and picnic areas are available for you to enjoy a meal or a snack surrounded by nature.

Water Activities: Depending on the season, you might see kayakers and white-water rafters navigating the Youghiogheny River.

Biking: The park also has biking trails, so you may encounter cyclists enjoying the beautiful scenery.

Wildlife: Keep an eye out for wildlife such as deer, birds, and other creatures that call the park home.

Before your drive, be sure to check the park's website for any trail closures or seasonal information. Whether you're a nature enthusiast, a photography buff, or someone seeking a relaxing scenic drive, Ohiopyle State Park offers a captivating and natural escape from the bustle of city life, making it a perfect day trip or weekend adventure from Pittsburgh.

51. Visit the Fort Pitt Museum.

Visiting the Fort Pitt Museum in Pittsburgh, Pennsylvania, is an opportunity to step back in time and explore the history of the region, particularly during the colonial and Revolutionary War periods. Here's what you can expect when you visit the Fort Pitt Museum:

Historical Significance: The museum is located at the site of Fort Pitt, a key fortification during the colonial era and the American Revolution, which played a pivotal role in the history of the region.

Exhibits and Artifacts: The museum features a wide range of exhibits and historical artifacts that provide insights into the fort's history, early American life, Native American cultures, and the broader context of the Revolutionary War.

Interactive Displays: Some exhibits offer interactive displays, allowing visitors to engage with the history and gain a deeper understanding of the past.

Artistic and Visual Representation: The museum often showcases art, illustrations, and visual representations of historical events, bringing the past to life.

Educational Programs: The Fort Pitt Museum offers educational programs, events, and workshops that focus on early American history and the history of the fort itself.

Fort Pitt Block House: Located nearby, the historic Fort Pitt Block House is one of the oldest surviving buildings in Western Pennsylvania. It's often included as part of the museum visit.

Panoramic Views: The museum's location provides panoramic views of downtown Pittsburgh and the surrounding landscape, offering an opportunity to appreciate the fort's strategic positioning.

Local History: The museum delves into the history of Pittsburgh, the role of Fort Pitt in the fur trade, Native American interactions, and the settlement of the region.

Cultural Context: You can learn about the diverse cultures and communities that inhabited the region during the 18th century and their interactions with one another.

Gift Shop: The museum typically has a gift shop where you can purchase books, historical reproductions, and souvenirs related to the fort and the history of the area.

Before your visit, it's a good idea to check the museum's website for current exhibitions, opening hours, and any special events or educational programs that may be taking place during your visit. Whether you're a history buff, a student, or someone looking to explore the history of Pittsburgh and the early United States, the Fort Pitt Museum offers a captivating and informative journey through the past.

52.Explore the historical reenactments at Bushy Run Battlefield.

Visiting Bushy Run Battlefield in Jeannette, Pennsylvania, offers an immersive experience of historical reenactments and a chance to learn about a pivotal event during the Pontiac's War in 1763. Here's what you can expect when you explore the historical reenactments at Bushy Run Battlefield:

Historical Significance: Bushy Run Battlefield is known for the Battle of Bushy Run, a significant conflict during Pontiac's War between Native American forces and British troops.

Reenactments: The battlefield hosts historical reenactments, bringing the events of 1763 to life. Reenactors in period costumes portray both British and Native American forces, providing an authentic look into the past.

Educational Programs: In addition to reenactments, the site offers educational programs and guided tours that delve into the history of the battle, the tactics used, and the broader historical context.

Living History: The reenactors often engage in living history, showcasing daily life, weaponry, and military drills of the 18th century. Visitors can interact with reenactors and gain insights into the era.

Battlefield Site: The battlefield itself provides a visual representation of the terrain where the battle took place, offering a deeper appreciation of the challenges faced by both sides.

Visitor Center: Bushy Run Battlefield's visitor center features exhibits, artifacts, and displays related to the battle and the history of the region.

Cultural Significance: The site explores the cultural exchange and conflicts between Native American tribes, British forces, and American settlers during the era.

Natural Beauty: The battlefield is set in a scenic, wooded area, providing opportunities for hiking and enjoying the natural surroundings in addition to learning about history.

Events and Festivals: The site hosts special events, festivals, and reenactment weekends that may include demonstrations, workshops, and cultural presentations.

Community Engagement: Bushy Run Battlefield is involved in the local community, offering educational programs and initiatives that celebrate the historical heritage of the region.

Before planning your visit, it's advisable to check the battlefield's website for information on reenactment schedules, educational programs, opening hours, and any special events or festivals that may be taking place during your visit. Whether you're a history enthusiast, a student of early American history, or someone interested in experiencing the past through reenactments, Bushy Run Battlefield offers a rich and engaging historical journey.

53.Attend a performance at the New Hazlett Theater.

Attending a performance at the New Hazlett Theater in Pittsburgh, Pennsylvania, offers an opportunity to experience a wide range of artistic and cultural events in an intimate and historic setting. Here's what you can expect when you attend a performance at the New Hazlett Theater:

Diverse Performances: The theater hosts a diverse array of performances, including theater productions, dance shows, music concerts, spoken word events, and other artistic presentations.

Local and International Artists: The theater showcases both local talents and international artists, offering a platform for emerging and established performers.

Intimate Setting: The New Hazlett Theater is known for its intimate and cozy atmosphere, providing an up-close and personal experience with the performers.

Variety of Genres: You can enjoy a variety of performance genres, from contemporary and experimental works to traditional and classical art forms.

Innovative Productions: The theater often features innovative and cutting-edge productions that challenge artistic boundaries and engage audiences with thought-provoking performances.

Cultural Engagement: Many performances touch on cultural and societal themes, making the theater a place for exploring contemporary issues through the arts.

Community Involvement: The New Hazlett Theater actively engages with the local community, offering educational programs, workshops, and events that promote arts and culture.

Special Events: The theater occasionally hosts special events, discussions, and panels related to the arts and the creative process.

Historic Venue: The theater is housed in a historic building with a rich history, which adds to the ambiance and character of the space.

Café and Lounge: The theater typically has a café or lounge area where you can enjoy refreshments and discuss the performance with fellow attendees before or after the show.

Before attending a performance, be sure to check the New Hazlett Theater's schedule for current productions, purchase tickets in advance, and explore any pre-show or post-show events that may enhance your experience. Whether you're an art enthusiast, a lover of the performing arts, or someone seeking a unique and cultural night out, the New Hazlett Theater offers an engaging and enriching artistic experience.

54.Take a scenic drive through Laurel Highlands (near Pittsburgh).

A scenic drive through the Laurel Highlands, located near Pittsburgh, Pennsylvania, is a breathtaking journey through the picturesque landscapes of the Appalachian Mountains. Here's what you can expect when you embark on a scenic drive through the Laurel Highlands:

Stunning Vistas: The Laurel Highlands offer some of the most captivating vistas in Pennsylvania, with rolling hills, dense forests, and scenic overlooks that provide panoramic views of the region.

Travel to Pittsburgh Pennsylvania

Lush Forests: As you drive through the region, you'll be surrounded by lush forests filled with hardwood trees, making it a delightful trip for nature enthusiasts, especially during the fall when the foliage turns vibrant shades of red, orange, and gold.

Historic Sites: The Laurel Highlands are home to several historic sites, including Fort Ligonier, which played a crucial role in early American history, and Fallingwater, Frank Lloyd Wright's architectural masterpiece.

Ohiopyle State Park: The drive may take you through or near Ohiopyle State Park, known for its natural beauty, waterfalls, and the Youghiogheny River. You can make a stop to explore the park's natural wonders and hiking trails.

Recreational Opportunities: The Laurel Highlands offer various recreational activities, from hiking and biking to fishing, picnicking, and birdwatching.

Unique Landscapes: The region features unique geological formations, such as the Laurel Caverns, which you can explore with guided tours.

Scenic Byways: There are designated scenic byways, such as the Laurel Highlands Scenic Byway, that offer the most breathtaking views and take you through some of the most beautiful parts of the region.

Small Towns: You'll encounter charming small towns with friendly residents, providing opportunities to stop for a meal, explore local shops, and experience the region's hospitality.

Art and Culture: The Laurel Highlands also boast a thriving arts and culture scene, with galleries, museums, and live performances that can be part of your journey.

Wildlife: Keep an eye out for wildlife, including deer, turkeys, and various bird species that inhabit the forests of the region.

Before your drive, consider checking the Laurel Highlands' official tourism website for recommendations on routes, scenic byways, attractions, and current conditions. Whether you're an outdoor enthusiast, a history buff, or someone looking to enjoy a leisurely and scenic drive, the Laurel Highlands offer a captivating and diverse natural and cultural landscape to explore.

55.Visit the Bayernhof Museum, a unique historic mansion.

Visiting the Bayernhof Museum in Pittsburgh, Pennsylvania, is a unique and fascinating experience, as it offers a glimpse into a historic mansion filled with an eclectic collection of art, music, and mechanical wonders. Here's what you can expect when you visit the Bayernhof Museum:

Historic Mansion: The museum is located within a stunning, Tudor-style mansion that dates back to the early 20th century. The architecture and interior design of the mansion are noteworthy in themselves.

Automated Music Machines: One of the main highlights of the museum is its extensive collection of automated music machines, including player pianos, orchestrions, and more. These machines play music from different eras and provide a unique auditory experience.

Antique Clocks: The Bayernhof Museum features an impressive collection of antique clocks and timepieces, with intricate designs and mechanisms.

Art and Decor: The mansion is adorned with a diverse assortment of art, decorative pieces, and furnishings from various time periods and cultures. The decor is eclectic and visually captivating.

Gardens and Grounds: The mansion is surrounded by beautifully landscaped gardens and terraces that offer peaceful areas to explore.

Guided Tours: Visitors typically take guided tours of the museum, providing insights into the history of the mansion, its owner, and the unique collection of items.

Musical Performances: Some tours may include live musical performances using the automated music machines, allowing you to experience the mansion's full auditory splendor.

Architectural and Engineering Wonders: The mansion features innovative architectural and engineering elements, including secret doors, hidden compartments, and other surprises.

Cultural and Historical Context: The museum's collection reflects the tastes, interests, and historical context of the mansion's owner, making it a fascinating journey through time.

Reservation Requirements: It's advisable to check the museum's website or contact them in advance to inquire about reservations, tour availability, and any special events.

Before your visit, be sure to check the Bayernhof Museum's website for information on tour schedules, ticket prices, and any special exhibitions or events that may be taking place during your visit. Whether you're an art connoisseur, a history buff, or simply someone with a curious spirit, the Bayernhof Museum provides a unique and immersive experience in the heart of Pittsburgh.

56.Explore the Frick Art & Historical Center.

Exploring the Frick Art & Historical Center in Pittsburgh, Pennsylvania, provides an opportunity to delve into the art, history, and culture of the Gilded Age through the impressive collections and the historic Frick family estate. Here's what you can expect when you visit the Frick Art & Historical Center:

Art Collections: The center features a remarkable collection of European paintings, including works by Old Masters like Vermeer, Rembrandt, and Gainsborough, as well as pieces by American artists such as John Singer Sargent and George Bellows.

Frick Family Estate: The center is housed within the Frick family estate, known as Clayton. You can explore the beautifully preserved mansion and its historic interiors, providing insights into the lifestyles of the wealthy during the Gilded Age.

Gardens and Grounds: The estate boasts meticulously maintained gardens and expansive grounds, offering a serene and picturesque environment for strolling and reflection.

Car and Carriage Museum: The Car and Carriage Museum features a collection of historic automobiles and carriages, showcasing transportation from the late 19th and early 20th centuries.

Educational Programs: The Frick Art & Historical Center offers educational programs, art classes, and workshops that cater to various age groups and interests.

Special Exhibitions: In addition to its permanent collections, the center hosts temporary exhibitions that explore a wide range of art and historical topics.

Family-Friendly Activities: The center often provides family-friendly programs, making it an ideal destination for visitors of all ages.

Art Conservation: You can witness art conservation in action, as the center's experts work to preserve and restore art pieces.

Historical Context: The center offers a window into the history of Pittsburgh and the social and industrial context of the Gilded Age.

Café and Gift Shop: You can enjoy refreshments at the café and explore the gift shop, which offers art-related merchandise and souvenirs.

Before your visit, it's a good idea to check the Frick Art & Historical Center's website for information on exhibitions, opening hours, admission fees, and any special events or programs that may be taking place during your visit. Whether you're an art enthusiast, a history lover, or someone looking for a tranquil and culturally enriching experience, the Frick Art & Historical Center offers a rich and varied journey through art, history, and the legacy of the Frick family.

57.Attend a live music performance at Club Cafe.

Attending a live music performance at Club Cafe in Pittsburgh, Pennsylvania, is a memorable experience that allows you to enjoy intimate and captivating musical performances in a cozy and welcoming venue. Here's what you can expect when you attend a live music performance at Club Cafe:

Intimate Setting: Club Cafe is known for its intimate and cozy atmosphere, providing an up-close and personal experience with the artists. It's a small and inviting venue that fosters a strong connection between musicians and the audience.

Diverse Music Acts: The venue hosts a wide range of music acts, including local, national, and international artists. You can enjoy live performances of various genres, from folk and indie rock to blues, jazz, and more.

Acoustic Excellence: The venue is designed with acoustics in mind, ensuring that the music sounds exceptional, and the artists' talents shine.

Local Talent: Club Cafe often showcases local and emerging musicians, making it a platform for supporting the local music scene and discovering new talent.

Music Variety: You may experience solo acoustic sets, full bands, singer-songwriters, and a diverse selection of musical styles, offering something for everyone.

Dining and Drinks: The venue typically offers a dining menu with a selection of food and drinks, allowing you to enjoy a meal or drinks before or during the performance.

Community Vibe: Club Cafe has a strong sense of community and is a popular gathering place for music enthusiasts and artists alike.

Small-Scale Performances: Because of the venue's size, you'll enjoy an up-close and personal connection with the artists and a sense of camaraderie with fellow concertgoers.

Late-Night Entertainment: Some performances take place in the evening or late at night, making Club Cafe an ideal choice for those looking for entertainment after dinner.

Special Events: The venue occasionally hosts special events, album release parties, and themed nights, adding excitement to the music calendar.

Before attending a performance, it's a good idea to check Club Cafe's website or social media channels for information on upcoming shows, ticket availability, and any special events or promotions. Whether you're a music enthusiast, a supporter of local artists, or someone seeking a relaxed and intimate live music experience, Club Cafe offers a vibrant and memorable night of entertainment.

58. Visit the Maridon Museum, dedicated to Asian art and culture.

Visiting the Maridon Museum in Butler, Pennsylvania, provides a unique opportunity to explore a diverse collection of Asian art and culture, including items from China and Japan. Here's what you can expect when you visit the Maridon Museum:

Asian Art Collections: The museum features a wide range of Asian art, including Chinese and Japanese ceramics, sculptures, paintings, textiles, and decorative arts. The collection spans centuries and offers a comprehensive look at Asian cultural and artistic traditions.

Chinese Jade and Snuff Bottle Collection: One of the highlights of the museum is its remarkable collection of Chinese jade, including intricately carved pieces. The snuff bottle collection showcases miniature works of art that were used for holding tobacco.

Japanese Netsuke: The museum is known for its extensive collection of Japanese netsuke, which are small carved sculptures that were used as toggles on traditional Japanese garments.

Exhibits and Displays: The museum's exhibits and displays are thoughtfully curated to provide historical and cultural context for the art and artifacts on view.

Educational Programs: The Maridon Museum offers educational programs and workshops that delve into Asian art, culture, and history. These programs are often engaging and informative for visitors of all ages.

Historical Context: The museum provides insights into the cultural and historical context of the Asian art, allowing visitors to appreciate the significance of the pieces on display.

Tea Room: The museum typically includes a traditional tea room where you can enjoy a tranquil moment and experience aspects of Asian tea culture.

Gardens: The museum often has gardens and outdoor spaces that offer a peaceful setting for reflection and relaxation.

Gift Shop: You can explore the museum's gift shop for books, souvenirs, and items related to Asian art and culture.

Before your visit, it's a good idea to check the Maridon Museum's website for information on opening hours, admission fees, special exhibitions, and any upcoming events or educational programs. Whether you're an art enthusiast, a student of Asian culture, or someone with a curious spirit, the Maridon Museum offers a captivating and educational journey through the rich and diverse world of Asian art and heritage.

59.Explore the Westmoreland Museum of American Art

Exploring the Westmoreland Museum of American Art in Greensburg, Pennsylvania, is a rich and culturally enriching experience that offers a comprehensive collection of American art. Here's what you can expect when you visit the Westmoreland Museum of American Art:

American Art Collection: The museum boasts a diverse and extensive collection of American art, featuring works from various time periods, styles, and regions. You can explore paintings, sculptures, decorative arts, and more.

Permanent Exhibits: The museum's permanent exhibits showcase American art history, spanning from colonial times to contemporary works. You'll encounter pieces that reflect the evolution of American art and culture.

Changing Exhibitions: In addition to its permanent collection, the museum hosts changing exhibitions that explore specific themes, artists, or artistic movements. These exhibits provide fresh and dynamic perspectives on American art.

Educational Programs: The Westmoreland Museum offers educational programs, art classes, and workshops for all ages, making it an ideal destination for learning and creativity.

Cultural Context: Many exhibits provide insights into the cultural, social, and historical context of the artworks, allowing visitors to gain a deeper understanding of the American experience.

Historical Artifacts: You'll find historical artifacts and decorative arts that provide a glimpse into daily life in America over the centuries.

Community Engagement: The museum actively engages with the local community, hosting events, lectures, and interactive programs that foster a deeper appreciation of American art.

Modern and Contemporary Art: While the museum has a strong emphasis on traditional American art, it also features modern and contemporary works that demonstrate the evolution of American artistic expression.

Art Conservation: The museum may have conservation labs or displays where visitors can learn about the preservation and restoration of artworks.

Museum Store: You can explore the museum store for books, prints, and unique art-related merchandise that make for memorable souvenirs.

Before your visit, it's a good idea to check the Westmoreland Museum of American Art's website for information on opening hours, admission fees, special exhibitions, and any upcoming events or programs. Whether you're an art enthusiast, a history buff, or someone looking to explore American culture through art, the Westmoreland Museum of American Art offers a rich and diverse journey through the creativity and heritage of the United States.

60.Attend a performance at the Pittsburgh Playhouse.

Attending a performance at the Pittsburgh Playhouse is a delightful and immersive experience, as it allows you to enjoy a wide range of theatrical and performing arts productions. Here's what you can expect when you attend a performance at the Pittsburgh Playhouse:

Diverse Performances: The Pittsburgh Playhouse hosts a diverse array of performances, including theater productions, musicals, dance shows, opera, and other live performing arts events.

Talented Performers: The performances often feature talented actors, singers, dancers, and musicians who bring stories to life on the stage.

Variety of Genres: You can enjoy a variety of theatrical genres, from classical and Shakespearean works to contemporary and experimental productions.

Intimate Setting: The Playhouse is known for its intimate and welcoming atmosphere, providing an up-close and personal experience with the performers and the stage.

Student and Professional Productions: The venue showcases both student productions from Point Park University's Conservatory of Performing Arts and professional performances, ensuring a diverse lineup of shows.

Costume and Set Design: You can expect elaborate and creative costume and set designs that enhance the storytelling and create immersive experiences.

Cultural and Social Themes: Many productions explore cultural, historical, and societal themes, making the theater a place for thought-provoking and engaging performances.

Educational Initiatives: The Pittsburgh Playhouse is actively involved in education and often offers workshops, classes, and outreach programs to foster the development of young talent and engage the community.

Special Events: The Playhouse occasionally hosts special events, such as opening night receptions, talkbacks with the cast and crew, and behind-the-scenes tours.

Café and Lounge: The theater often includes a café or lounge area where you can enjoy refreshments, wine, or light snacks before or after the performance.

Before attending a performance, it's a good idea to check the Pittsburgh Playhouse's website for information on current productions, ticket availability, and any special events or educational programs associated with the performances. Whether you're a theater enthusiast, a lover of the performing arts, or someone looking for a night of entertainment and culture, the Pittsburgh Playhouse offers an engaging and memorable experience in the heart of Pittsburgh.

61.Take a self-guided architectural walking tour in Oakland.

Taking a self-guided architectural walking tour in Oakland, a neighborhood in Pittsburgh, Pennsylvania, allows you to explore a wide range of architectural styles and historic buildings. Here's a suggested walking tour route, along with notable architectural highlights you can expect to encounter in Oakland:

Cathedral of Learning: Start your tour at the Cathedral of Learning on the University of Pittsburgh's campus. This iconic skyscraper is a prime example of Gothic Revival architecture and serves as the centerpiece of the university. Don't forget to check out the Nationality Rooms inside, which showcase different international architectural styles.

Heinz Memorial Chapel: Continue to Heinz Memorial Chapel, a stunning neo-Gothic structure that features intricate stained glass windows and a grand interior.

Stephen Foster Memorial: Walk to the Stephen Foster Memorial, which houses the Center for American Music and is known for its Beaux-Arts architecture and decorative elements.

Soldiers and Sailors Memorial Hall: This grand neoclassical building is a memorial to American military veterans. It's worth exploring the exterior and reading the inscriptions.

Carnegie Library of Pittsburgh - Main Branch: The Carnegie Library, designed in a Beaux-Arts style by architects Alden & Harlow, is a beautiful and historically significant structure.

Frick Fine Arts Building: Head to the Frick Fine Arts Building, a striking neoclassical structure that houses the University of Pittsburgh's School of Arts and Sciences.

Forbes Field Wall: While the original Forbes Field no longer stands, you can visit the preserved outfield wall of the historic baseball stadium, which played a significant role in Pittsburgh's sports history.

Phipps Conservatory and Botanical Gardens: Though not known for its architecture, Phipps Conservatory is a beautiful and historic glasshouse where you can enjoy lush greenery and botanical wonders.

Schenley Farms Historic District: As you continue walking, you'll notice an array of architectural styles, including Tudor, Victorian, and Colonial Revival, in the Schenley Farms Historic District. Admire the well-preserved homes in this area.

University of Pittsburgh's Campus: Stroll through the University of Pittsburgh's campus to see more examples of collegiate Gothic and modern architectural styles, such as the Hillman Library.

Oakland Square: End your tour at Oakland Square, a vibrant public space surrounded by a mix of historic and modern structures. This is a great place to relax and reflect on your architectural exploration.

Before embarking on your self-guided tour, consider researching the opening hours and accessibility of the various sites. Be sure to take your time and soak in the architectural beauty and history of Oakland.

62. Visit the West End Overlook for panoramic city views.

Visiting the West End Overlook in Pittsburgh, Pennsylvania, offers breathtaking panoramic views of the city and its stunning skyline. Here's what you can expect when you visit the West End Overlook:

Spectacular Views: The West End Overlook provides some of the most stunning and iconic views of the Pittsburgh skyline. You'll have a sweeping vista of the city's downtown, bridges, and the three rivers (the Allegheny, Monongahela, and Ohio).

Photo Opportunities: The overlook is a popular spot for photography enthusiasts and tourists alike. The unique vantage point allows for capturing memorable shots of the cityscape, especially during sunrise and sunset.

Peaceful Setting: The overlook offers a serene and peaceful environment, making it an ideal place for quiet reflection, enjoying a picnic, or simply taking in the beauty of the city.

Historical Significance: The West End Overlook has historical significance and is known as one of the key scenic viewpoints in Pittsburgh. It's been a favorite spot for locals and visitors for generations.

Local Landmark: The overlook is a beloved local landmark, often featured in films, television shows, and postcards. It's a great way to get a sense of Pittsburgh's unique topography.

Benches and Picnic Tables: The site provides benches and picnic tables, making it a comfortable place to relax and soak in the views.

Ample Parking: There's usually ample parking available at the overlook, making it easy to access and enjoy the view without hassle.

Nearby Parks: The West End Overlook is situated near parks like the Sheraden Park and the West End-Elliott Overlook Park, providing additional opportunities for outdoor activities and exploration.

Accessibility: The overlook is typically wheelchair-accessible, allowing people of all abilities to enjoy the views.

Sunrise and Sunset: Consider visiting the West End Overlook at sunrise or sunset to witness the city transform with dramatic colors and the play of light on the rivers.

Before your visit, check the West End Overlook's official website or local information sources for any special events, operating hours, and any restrictions that may be in place. Whether you're a photography enthusiast, a lover of scenic views, or someone seeking a peaceful place to contemplate the city's beauty, the West End Overlook is a must-visit destination in Pittsburgh.

63.Explore the Pittsburgh Vintage Grand Prix.

Exploring the Pittsburgh Vintage Grand Prix is an exciting and unique experience that combines classic car racing with charitable fundraising. Here's what you can expect when you attend this event:

Historic Race Cars: The Pittsburgh Vintage Grand Prix (PVGP) features a wide range of historic race cars, including vintage sports cars, open-wheel racers, and exotic automobiles. You'll get to see these beautiful machines up close.

Spectacular Races: The PVGP hosts competitive vintage car races on the city's challenging streets, creating a thrilling spectacle for motorsport enthusiasts. It's a rare opportunity to witness classic cars racing at high speeds in an urban setting.

Travel to Pittsburgh Pennsylvania

Car Shows: In addition to the races, there are various car shows where classic car enthusiasts showcase their vehicles. You'll find an impressive array of vintage automobiles from different eras, each lovingly restored and maintained.

Concours d'Elegance: The PVGP often features a Concours d'Elegance, an elegant display of the most exceptional and beautifully restored classic cars. It's a highlight for admirers of automotive artistry.

Charitable Cause: The PVGP is not just about cars; it's also a charitable event. The Grand Prix has raised millions of dollars for the Autism Society of Pittsburgh and the Allegheny Valley School over the years. Your attendance supports these causes.

Family-Friendly Activities: The event typically offers family-friendly activities such as a car cruise, parades, and entertainment options for all ages.

Food and Vendors: You can enjoy a variety of food vendors, car-related merchandise, and automotive memorabilia.

Community Engagement: The PVGP is deeply rooted in the local community, and the event often includes local businesses, car clubs, and enthusiasts who come together to celebrate classic cars.

Education and Awareness: The PVGP promotes automotive education and awareness, making it an educational experience for car enthusiasts and the general public.

Historic Location: The event takes place in Schenley Park, offering a picturesque and historic setting for a day of vintage car racing and appreciation.

Before attending the Pittsburgh Vintage Grand Prix, check the official event website for dates, schedule, ticket information, and any specific details regarding races, car shows, and activities. Whether you're a classic car enthusiast, a motorsport fan, or someone interested in supporting charitable causes, the Pittsburgh Vintage Grand Prix offers a thrilling and charitable celebration of automotive history.

64.Attend a show at the Arcade Comedy Theater.

Attending a show at the Arcade Comedy Theater in Pittsburgh, Pennsylvania, promises an evening filled with laughter and entertainment. Here's what you can expect when you attend a show at this comedy theater:

Improv and Sketch Comedy: The Arcade Comedy Theater specializes in improv and sketch comedy, providing a stage for talented comedians to showcase their improvisational skills and scripted sketches.

Live Performances: You'll have the opportunity to watch live comedy performances featuring local and touring comedians. These shows often include audience interaction and participation, making each performance unique and unpredictable.

Variety of Acts: The theater hosts a variety of acts, including short-form and long-form improv, stand-up comedy, storytelling, and comedy troupes. The diverse lineup ensures there's something for everyone's sense of humor.

Intimate Setting: The theater's intimate and cozy setting allows for an up-close and personal comedy experience. The audience's proximity to the stage creates an engaging and interactive atmosphere.

Talented Comedians: You'll enjoy performances by skilled comedians who excel in quick wit and humor, creating an atmosphere of laughter and amusement.

Local Talent: The theater often showcases local comedians, supporting and promoting the vibrant comedy scene in Pittsburgh.

Late-Night Entertainment: Some shows are scheduled in the evening or late at night, making the Arcade Comedy Theater a great choice for post-dinner entertainment.

Refreshments: The theater may offer a selection of snacks and beverages to enjoy during the show.

Audience Participation: Many comedy acts encourage audience participation, so be prepared to be part of the laughter and fun.

Special Events: The theater occasionally hosts special events, themed shows, and workshops, enhancing the comedy experience.

Before attending a show, check the Arcade Comedy Theater's website for information on show schedules, ticket availability, and any special events or themed performances that may be taking place. Whether you're a comedy enthusiast, a fan of improvisational humor, or someone looking for a night of laughter and entertainment, the Arcade Comedy Theater offers a lively and enjoyable comedy experience in the heart of Pittsburgh.

65. Take a scenic drive through Forbes State Forest (near Pittsburgh).

Taking a scenic drive through Forbes State Forest, located near Pittsburgh, Pennsylvania, is a tranquil and immersive experience in nature. Here's what you can expect when you embark on a scenic drive through this beautiful forest:

Spectacular Landscapes: Forbes State Forest covers a vast area of lush woodlands, rolling hills, and serene valleys. As you drive through, you'll encounter breathtaking natural beauty.

Diverse Flora and Fauna: The forest is home to a wide variety of plant and animal species. Keep an eye out for wildlife like deer, turkey, and various bird species, as well as diverse plant life.

Scenic Byways: There are designated scenic byways and roads that guide you through the forest, offering the most picturesque views and allowing you to fully appreciate the natural landscape.

Hiking Trails: Forbes State Forest features numerous hiking trails that you can explore along the way. These trails provide opportunities for short walks, day hikes, or more extended backpacking adventures.

Camping Sites: If you're interested in camping, the forest offers campgrounds and campsites where you can set up tents or park an RV.

Picnic Areas: There are often designated picnic areas with tables and grills, allowing you to stop for a meal and enjoy the forest's tranquility.

Fishing: If you're an angler, there are streams and lakes within the forest where you can try your hand at fishing.

Birdwatching: Forbes State Forest is a great place for birdwatching, with opportunities to spot both resident and migratory bird species.

Fall Foliage: In the autumn, the forest's foliage transforms into a vibrant display of red, orange, and yellow, making it a popular spot for leaf-peeping.

Natural Springs and Scenic Overlooks: Along your drive, you may encounter natural springs and scenic overlooks that provide even more opportunities to connect with nature and capture stunning views.

Before your scenic drive, it's a good idea to check the Forbes State Forest's official website for information on road conditions, trails, camping, and any seasonal events or guided activities that may be taking place. Whether you're a nature enthusiast, a hiker, or someone looking for a peaceful escape from the city, Forbes State Forest offers a serene and picturesque journey through the natural beauty of Western Pennsylvania.

66. Visit the Tull Family Theater, an independent cinema.

Visiting the Tull Family Theater in Sewickley, Pennsylvania, is a fantastic way to enjoy independent and mainstream films in a welcoming and community-oriented setting. Here's what you can expect when you visit this independent cinema:

Film Screenings: The Tull Family Theater screens a diverse selection of films, including independent, foreign, documentary, and mainstream movies. You'll have the opportunity to watch a wide range of cinematic experiences.

Art House Ambiance: The theater often boasts an art house ambiance, offering a unique and cozy setting for film lovers. It provides an intimate atmosphere that's perfect for enjoying movies.

Community Engagement: The theater is deeply engaged with the local community and often hosts events, discussions, and Q&A sessions with filmmakers. This fosters a sense of community and encourages discussions about cinema.

Film Festivals: The Tull Family Theater occasionally hosts film festivals and special events, showcasing a curated selection of films that cater to different interests and themes.

Educational Programs: The theater offers educational programs for all ages, including film workshops, discussions, and opportunities to learn more about the art and craft of filmmaking.

Local Talent: The theater may screen films created by local filmmakers or films that showcase local talent, providing support for the regional film industry.

Café and Concessions: You can enjoy a selection of snacks, drinks, and refreshments, creating a complete cinema experience.

Cozy Seating: The theater often provides comfortable and well-maintained seating, allowing you to relax and enjoy the films in comfort.

Accessible and Inclusive: The Tull Family Theater is generally accessible to people with disabilities and aims to be an inclusive space for all moviegoers.

Support for Independent Film: By visiting the Tull Family Theater, you support the independent film industry and contribute to the cultural vibrancy of the local community.

Before attending a screening, check the theater's official website for information on showtimes, ticket prices, and any special events, festivals, or guest appearances. Whether you're a cinephile, an advocate for independent cinema, or someone looking for a unique cinematic experience, the Tull Family Theater offers a welcoming and culturally enriching venue for enjoying the art of film.

67.Explore the historic Hartwood Acres Park and Mansion.

Exploring Hartwood Acres Park and Mansion in Allegheny County, near Pittsburgh, offers a delightful blend of natural beauty and historic architecture. Here's what you can expect when you visit this picturesque estate:

Hartwood Acres Park:

Spectacular Grounds: The park encompasses 629 acres of lush greenery, including woodlands, meadows, and open fields. You'll have ample space to explore and enjoy the great outdoors.

Trails: Hartwood Acres Park offers a network of scenic hiking and walking trails, providing opportunities for both leisurely strolls and more challenging hikes. The trails are perfect for nature lovers and outdoor enthusiasts.

Picnic Areas: The park features designated picnic areas where you can enjoy an outdoor meal with friends or family. The serene setting and well-maintained facilities make it an ideal spot for a picnic.

Concerts and Events: Hartwood Acres is known for hosting outdoor concerts and events during the summer months. The outdoor amphitheater often showcases a diverse range of musical performances, attracting visitors from near and far.

Playgrounds: If you have children, there are playgrounds and play areas where they can have fun and burn off some energy.

Winter Activities: During the winter, the park provides opportunities for cross-country skiing, sledding, and other cold-weather activities.

Scenic Overlook: There's a scenic overlook that offers captivating views of the park and the surrounding landscape, perfect for photo opportunities.

Hartwood Acres Mansion:

Historic Mansion: The Hartwood Acres Mansion is a Tudor-style mansion that was once a private residence. Today, it serves as a cultural center and is open for guided tours.

Architectural Splendor: The mansion features exquisite architectural details, including beautiful woodwork, stained glass windows, and period furnishings. You'll get to explore the rich history and heritage of the estate.

Guided Tours: Trained guides often lead tours through the mansion, providing insights into its history, the families who lived there, and the cultural significance of the building.

Special Events: The mansion occasionally hosts special events, art exhibitions, and cultural programs, adding depth and cultural enrichment to your visit.

Before your visit, check the official website or local information sources for details on park hours, guided tours of the mansion, special events, and any seasonal activities that may be taking place. Whether you're a nature enthusiast, a history buff, a music lover, or someone looking for a serene and culturally enriching experience, Hartwood Acres Park and Mansion offers a well-rounded visit that celebrates both the beauty of nature and the heritage of the region.

68.Attend a performance by the Pittsburgh New Music Ensemble.

Attending a performance by the Pittsburgh New Music Ensemble (PNME) is an exciting and innovative musical experience that celebrates contemporary and avant-garde compositions. Here's what you can expect when you attend a PNME performance:

Contemporary Music: The Pittsburgh New Music Ensemble focuses on performing contemporary classical music, showcasing the work of living composers. You'll have the opportunity to hear cutting-edge compositions that push the boundaries of traditional classical music.

World Premieres: PNME often features world premieres of new compositions, providing an exclusive opportunity to be among the first to hear groundbreaking works.

Diverse Repertoire: The ensemble's repertoire includes a wide range of musical styles, from experimental and avant-garde pieces to more accessible contemporary compositions.

Talented Musicians: PNME features a group of highly skilled and accomplished musicians who excel in performing challenging and unconventional works.

Intimate Settings: Performances by the Pittsburgh New Music Ensemble often take place in intimate and acoustically well-suited venues, creating an immersive and engaging listening experience.

Educational and Informative: Many performances are accompanied by pre-concert talks or discussions with composers and musicians, enhancing your understanding of the music and the creative process.

Collaborations: The ensemble frequently collaborates with other artists, including visual artists, choreographers, and multimedia artists, resulting in multisensory and interdisciplinary performances.

Experimental Instruments: You may encounter unconventional and experimental instruments, electronic elements, and unique musical techniques that challenge traditional notions of orchestration.

Seasonal Themes: PNME often organizes performances around thematic concepts, exploring topics, stories, or social issues through music.

Support for Contemporary Composers: By attending PNME performances, you support the work of contemporary composers and contribute to the vitality of new music.

Before attending a performance, check the Pittsburgh New Music Ensemble's official website or local event listings for information on concert schedules, ticket availability, and any special events or collaborations. Whether you're a fan of contemporary classical music, an aficionado of experimental sounds, or someone looking for a musically adventurous experience, the Pittsburgh New Music Ensemble offers a dynamic and thought-provoking journey into the world of modern compositions.

69. Take a scenic drive through Chestnut Ridge Park (near Pittsburgh).

Taking a scenic drive through Chestnut Ridge Park, located near Pittsburgh, Pennsylvania, offers a peaceful and immersive experience in the beauty of nature. Here's what you can expect when you embark on a scenic drive through this picturesque park:

Lush Woodlands: Chestnut Ridge Park is known for its dense woodlands, providing a serene and natural environment. The park's forested areas are especially striking during the fall when the leaves change color.

Picnic Areas: There are designated picnic areas within the park, making it an ideal spot to stop and enjoy an outdoor meal with friends or family.

Hiking Trails: While driving, you may come across trailheads for hiking and walking trails. These trails provide opportunities for exploring the park on foot and appreciating its natural beauty up close.

Wildlife: The park is home to a variety of wildlife, including deer, birds, and other creatures. Keep your eyes peeled for potential wildlife sightings.

Scenic Overlooks: There are often scenic overlooks within the park that offer beautiful views of the surrounding landscape. These vantage points provide opportunities for photography and enjoying the natural beauty.

Camping: Depending on the season and park regulations, you may have the option to camp within Chestnut Ridge Park. Camping facilities and campsites are usually well-maintained.

Sledding and Winter Activities: During the winter months, the park provides opportunities for sledding, snowshoeing, and cross-country skiing.

Spring Blooms: In the spring, you'll likely encounter vibrant wildflowers and blossoming trees, adding color and vibrancy to the park's scenery.

Peaceful Environment: Chestnut Ridge Park offers a peaceful and serene environment for relaxation and connection with nature.

Before your scenic drive, it's a good idea to check the park's official website or local information sources for details on road conditions, seasonal activities, and any specific park rules or guidelines that may be in place. Whether you're a nature enthusiast, a hiker, or someone seeking a peaceful escape from the city, Chestnut Ridge Park offers a beautiful and refreshing journey through the natural beauty of Western Pennsylvania.

70. Visit the Todd Nature Reserve in Sarver (near Pittsburgh).

Visiting the Todd Nature Reserve in Sarver, located near Pittsburgh, Pennsylvania, offers a serene and immersive experience in the beauty of the natural world. Here's what you can expect when you explore this picturesque reserve:

Todd Nature Reserve:

Scenic Nature Trails: The Todd Nature Reserve features well-maintained nature trails that wind through lush woodlands, providing opportunities for leisurely walks, hiking, birdwatching, and nature exploration.

Diverse Ecosystems: The reserve encompasses diverse ecosystems, including forests, wetlands, meadows, and streams. You can observe a wide variety of plant and animal species in their natural habitats.

Educational Signage: Along the trails, you may find educational signage that provides information about the local flora and fauna, as well as the natural history of the region.

Birdwatching: The reserve is a haven for birdwatchers, with opportunities to spot numerous bird species. Don't forget to bring your binoculars and a birding guide.

Photography: The natural beauty of the reserve offers excellent opportunities for nature photography. Capture the scenic landscapes, native wildlife, and the changing seasons.

Peaceful Setting: The reserve provides a peaceful and tranquil environment for quiet reflection and relaxation, making it a perfect spot for those seeking solitude and connection with nature.

Wildlife: Keep an eye out for wildlife such as deer, turtles, frogs, and various songbirds. It's not uncommon to encounter animals going about their daily routines.

Seasonal Changes: The reserve's beauty varies with the seasons. You can expect vibrant spring blooms, lush summer foliage, colorful fall foliage, and serene winter landscapes.

Nature Programs: The Todd Nature Reserve may offer educational programs, guided hikes, and nature-related events throughout the year. These programs enhance your understanding of the local ecosystem.

Accessible Trails: Some of the trails are often wheelchair-accessible, ensuring that the reserve is open to visitors of all abilities.

Before your visit, it's a good idea to check the Todd Nature Reserve's official website or local information sources for details on trail conditions, seasonal activities, and any specific guidelines or regulations in place. Whether you're a nature enthusiast, a hiker, a birdwatcher, or someone looking for a peaceful and natural escape, the Todd Nature Reserve offers a captivating and rejuvenating journey through the wonders of Western Pennsylvania's natural world.

71.Explore the Pittsburgh Cultural Trust Gallery Crawl.

Exploring the Pittsburgh Cultural Trust Gallery Crawl is a vibrant and immersive experience in the world of visual arts and culture. Here's what you can expect when you attend this exciting event:

Gallery Crawl by Pittsburgh Cultural Trust:

Visual Arts Exhibitions: The Gallery Crawl features a diverse array of visual art exhibitions. You can explore galleries, art studios, and exhibition spaces throughout the Cultural District, each showcasing unique and thought-provoking works of art.

Variety of Art Forms: The event often includes a wide range of artistic expressions, from painting, sculpture, and photography to new media, digital art, and installations. You'll encounter a variety of art forms and styles.

Local and International Artists: The Gallery Crawl provides a platform for both local and international artists to showcase their creations. It's an opportunity to discover emerging talents and established artists.

Interactive Installations: Some exhibitions feature interactive and multimedia installations that engage the senses and encourage audience participation.

Live Performances: The Cultural Trust often incorporates live performances into the Crawl, including music, dance, theater, and spoken word. These performances add a dynamic and multisensory dimension to the event.

Art Talks and Workshops: You may have the chance to attend art talks, workshops, and panel discussions led by artists and curators. These sessions offer insights into the creative process and artistic concepts.

Gallery Openings: Many galleries use the Gallery Crawl as an opportunity to open new exhibitions and debut new collections.

Art for Sale: If you're an art collector or enthusiast, you'll find some pieces available for purchase, allowing you to acquire unique artwork for your collection.

Food and Refreshments: The event often includes food trucks, vendors, and dining options, providing a chance to enjoy local cuisine and refreshments.

Family-Friendly Activities: The Gallery Crawl is typically family-friendly and may include activities and art projects for children, making it an ideal outing for families.

Before attending the Gallery Crawl, check the Pittsburgh Cultural Trust's official website or local event listings for information on event dates, participating galleries and venues, and any specific programming or special exhibitions that may be taking place. Whether you're an art lover, a cultural enthusiast, or someone looking for an engaging and immersive experience in the arts, the Gallery Crawl offers a dynamic and enriching journey through Pittsburgh's vibrant arts and culture scene.

72.Attend a performance by Attack Theatre.

Attending a performance by Attack Theatre is a captivating and innovative experience that combines dance, theater, and multimedia to create dynamic and thought-provoking productions. Here's what you can expect when you attend a performance by Attack Theatre:

Contemporary Dance: Attack Theatre is known for its contemporary dance performances that push the boundaries of traditional dance forms. You'll witness dancers who are skilled in a variety of movement styles and techniques.

Multi-Disciplinary Art: The theater often incorporates elements of theater, multimedia, and technology to create a multi-disciplinary and immersive artistic experience.

Original Works: Attack Theatre produces original and cutting-edge works of art that are both visually stunning and conceptually challenging.

Collaborations: The theater frequently collaborates with other artists, including musicians, visual artists, and multimedia designers, resulting in performances that merge multiple art forms.

Innovative Choreography: You'll be treated to innovative choreography that tells stories, explores themes, and conveys emotions in unique and unexpected ways.

Live Music: Many performances are accompanied by live music, adding a live and rhythmic dimension to the dance experience.

Engaging Storytelling: Attack Theatre often weaves narratives and storytelling into their performances, engaging the audience on an emotional and intellectual level.

Visual and Theatrical Effects: The theater employs visual and theatrical effects, such as lighting, projections, and set design, to create stunning and immersive environments.

Community Engagement: Attack Theatre is deeply engaged with the local community and often hosts educational programs, workshops, and outreach events that enhance the audience's understanding of dance and the creative process.

Varied Repertoire: The theater's repertoire includes a wide range of works, from abstract and experimental pieces to narrative and emotionally charged performances.

Before attending a performance, check the Attack Theatre's official website or local event listings for information on show schedules, ticket availability, and any special events, collaborations, or workshops that may be taking place. Whether you're a dance enthusiast, a lover of contemporary art, or someone seeking a visually captivating and intellectually stimulating experience, Attack Theatre offers a dynamic and thought-provoking journey into the world of contemporary dance and multi-disciplinary performance art.

73.Take a scenic drive through McConnell's Mill State Park (near Pittsburgh).

Taking a scenic drive through McConnell's Mill State Park, located near Pittsburgh, Pennsylvania, offers a beautiful and immersive experience in the great outdoors. Here's what you can expect when you embark on a scenic drive through this picturesque park:

McConnell's Mill State Park:

Spectacular Landscapes: The park encompasses 2,546 acres of stunning natural beauty, featuring deep gorges, unique rock formations, and dense woodlands. Your drive will take you through a variety of captivating landscapes.

Slippery Rock Creek: The park is situated along the Slippery Rock Creek, and your drive may offer glimpses of the winding creek and its cascading waterfalls, providing serene and picturesque views.

Hiking Trails: While driving through the park, you'll encounter trailheads for hiking and walking trails. These trails are perfect for exploration on foot and can lead you to some of the park's most iconic natural features.

Scenic Overlooks: The park features several scenic overlooks that provide breathtaking views of the gorges, cliffs, and the surrounding landscape. These overlooks offer excellent photo opportunities.

Picnic Areas: There are designated picnic areas where you can stop and enjoy a meal in the midst of nature. The sounds of the flowing creek add to the peaceful ambiance.

Rock Climbing: McConnell's Mill is a popular spot for rock climbing and bouldering, and you might spot climbers scaling the unique rock formations as you drive through the park.

Historic Gristmill: The park is home to a historic gristmill, McConnell's Mill, which you can visit and explore. The mill provides a glimpse into the region's industrial history.

Wildlife: Keep an eye out for wildlife such as deer, turkey, and a variety of bird species. The park offers opportunities for wildlife sightings.

Changing Seasons: The park's beauty varies with the seasons. Spring brings blossoming wildflowers, while the fall offers vibrant foliage and cool, refreshing air.

Cross-Country Skiing: During the winter months, the park provides opportunities for cross-country skiing, offering a serene and snowy landscape for winter enthusiasts.

Before your scenic drive, it's a good idea to check the McConnell's Mill State Park's official website or local information sources for details on road conditions, trail access, and any specific park rules or regulations in place. Whether you're a nature enthusiast, a history buff, or someone seeking a peaceful escape in the outdoors, McConnell's Mill State Park offers a captivating and rejuvenating journey through the natural beauty of Western Pennsylvania.

74. Visit the Southern Alleghenies Museum of Art (in Ligonier, near Pittsburgh).

Visiting the Southern Alleghenies Museum of Art in Ligonier, near Pittsburgh, Pennsylvania, offers a wonderful opportunity to immerse yourself in visual arts and cultural experiences. Here's what you can expect when you visit this museum:

Southern Alleghenies Museum of Art:

Art Exhibitions: The museum hosts a rotating collection of art exhibitions featuring a diverse range of works, including paintings, sculptures, photography, and other visual arts. You'll have the chance to explore various artistic styles and periods.

Local and Regional Art: The museum often emphasizes local and regional artists, showcasing the talent and creativity of the Alleghenies and surrounding areas.

Permanent Collection: The museum may house a permanent collection of artworks that provide insight into the artistic heritage of the region and highlight significant artists and art movements.

Educational Programs: The museum frequently offers educational programs, workshops, and lectures that enhance your understanding of art and its cultural significance. These programs are suitable for visitors of all ages.

Gallery Spaces: You'll be able to wander through gallery spaces with well-curated exhibitions that encourage appreciation and engagement with the artworks.

Community Involvement: The Southern Alleghenies Museum of Art is deeply involved with the local community and may collaborate with schools, artists, and cultural organizations to promote arts and culture in the region.

Art for Sale: If you're an art collector or enthusiast, some artworks on display may be available for purchase, allowing you to add unique pieces to your collection.

Special Events: The museum often hosts special events, openings, and receptions to celebrate new exhibitions and foster a sense of community among art lovers.

Cultural Enrichment: By visiting the museum, you contribute to the cultural vibrancy of the region and support the preservation and promotion of the visual arts.

Before your visit, check the Southern Alleghenies Museum of Art's official website or local event listings for information on museum hours, current exhibitions, admission fees, and any special events or programs that may be taking place. Whether you're an art enthusiast, a cultural explorer, or someone looking for a stimulating and visually enriching experience, the Southern Alleghenies Museum of Art offers a rewarding journey through the world of visual arts and cultural heritage in Western Pennsylvania.

75.Explore the Pittsburgh Glass Art Studio.

Exploring the Pittsburgh Glass Center (PGC) offers a unique and creative experience in the world of glass art. Here's what you can expect when you visit this vibrant studio:

Pittsburgh Glass Center:

Wildlife: Keep an eye out for wildlife such as deer, turkey, and a variety of bird species. The park provides opportunities for wildlife sightings.

Changing Seasons: The park's beauty varies with the seasons. Spring brings blossoming wildflowers, while the fall offers vibrant foliage and cool, refreshing air.

Historical Sites: Beaver Creek State Park features historical sites, including the remnants of the 19th-century Gaston's Mill and the restored pioneer village of Pioneer Village.

Recreational Activities: Depending on the season and park regulations, you may have the option to enjoy activities such as hiking, birdwatching, fishing, and hunting.

Before your scenic drive, it's a good idea to check the Beaver Creek State Park's official website or local information sources for details on road conditions, seasonal activities, and any specific park rules or guidelines that may be in place. Whether you're a nature enthusiast, a history buff, or someone seeking a peaceful escape in the outdoors, Beaver Creek State Park offers a captivating and rejuvenating journey through the natural beauty of Western Pennsylvania.

78. Visit the Westmoreland Heritage Trail (near Pittsburgh).

Visiting the Westmoreland Heritage Trail near Pittsburgh, Pennsylvania, offers an enjoyable and active outdoor experience through scenic natural and historical landscapes. Here's what you can expect when you explore this delightful trail:

Westmoreland Heritage Trail:

Scenic Beauty: The Westmoreland Heritage Trail provides a scenic and picturesque route through Western Pennsylvania's natural landscapes. You'll encounter lush greenery, serene waterways, and various points of interest along the way.

Historical Significance: The trail often passes through or near sites with historical significance, allowing you to connect with the area's heritage and past.

Special Events: The theater may host special events, receptions, and discussions with the cast and creative team, offering a chance to connect with fellow theater enthusiasts and artists.

Before attending a performance, check Quantum Theatre's official website or local event listings for information on show schedules, ticket availability, and any special events or site-specific locations that may be taking place. Whether you're a theater aficionado, a lover of avant-garde art, or someone seeking a unique and immersive theatrical experience, Quantum Theatre offers a dynamic and thought-provoking journey into the world of innovative theater and storytelling.

77.Take a scenic drive through Beaver Creek State Park (near Pittsburgh).

Taking a scenic drive through Beaver Creek State Park, located near Pittsburgh, Pennsylvania, offers a peaceful and immersive experience in the beauty of nature. Here's what you can expect when you embark on a scenic drive through this picturesque park:

Beaver Creek State Park:

Tranquil Landscapes: Beaver Creek State Park encompasses 2,722 acres of natural beauty, featuring woodlands, meadows, and wetlands. Your drive will take you through a variety of captivating landscapes.

Beaver Creek: The park is named after Beaver Creek, and you'll have the opportunity to see the creek, which winds through the park's scenic landscape.

Scenic Overlooks: The park offers several scenic overlooks that provide stunning views of the rolling hills, valleys, and woodlands, making for excellent photo opportunities.

Picnic Areas: There are designated picnic areas within the park where you can stop and enjoy a meal amidst the tranquil surroundings.

Hiking Trails: While driving, you'll encounter trailheads for hiking and walking trails, allowing you to explore the park on foot and appreciate its natural beauty up close.

76.Attend a performance by Quantum Theatre.

Attending a performance by Quantum Theatre is an immersive and innovative theatrical experience that takes you on a journey to unique and unexpected locations. Here's what you can expect when you attend a Quantum Theatre performance:

Quantum Theatre:

Site-Specific Performances: Quantum Theatre is known for staging site-specific productions in unconventional and non-traditional locations, such as abandoned buildings, gardens, historic sites, and more. You can expect to be transported to intriguing and unexpected settings that become integral parts of the storytelling.

Cutting-Edge Theater: The theater produces contemporary and thought-provoking plays, often showcasing new works and adaptations. You'll encounter innovative and experimental theater that challenges conventional norms.

Multidisciplinary Approach: Quantum Theatre often integrates various art forms, including visual art, music, dance, and multimedia, into its productions, creating a multisensory and immersive theatrical experience.

Intimate Performances: The theater's site-specific approach often results in intimate and immersive performances, allowing you to feel deeply connected to the narrative and characters.

Unique Artistic Collaborations: Quantum Theatre frequently collaborates with local and international artists, designers, and creative teams, resulting in productions that push the boundaries of traditional theater.

Engaging Storytelling: The theater is committed to telling engaging stories that explore complex themes and narratives. You'll have the opportunity to experience thought-provoking and emotionally charged performances.

Community Engagement: Quantum Theatre is deeply engaged with the local community and often hosts educational programs, discussions, and outreach events that enhance your understanding of the creative process and the themes of the productions.

Travel to Pittsburgh Pennsylvania

Glass Art Exhibitions: The Pittsburgh Glass Center often hosts rotating exhibitions that showcase a wide range of glass art, from traditional to contemporary. You'll have the opportunity to view exquisite glass sculptures, vessels, and installations.

Working Studios: The center includes working studios where resident and visiting artists create their glass artworks. You can observe the glassblowing and glassmaking process up close, gaining insight into the artistry and craftsmanship involved.

Educational Programs: PGC is dedicated to education and offers a variety of glass art classes and workshops for all skill levels, from beginners to experienced artists. You can take classes in glassblowing, flameworking, fusing, and kiln casting.

Glassblowing Demonstrations: The center often hosts glassblowing demonstrations, which provide an opportunity to watch skilled artists shape molten glass into beautiful and intricate forms.

Glass Art Supplies: PGC has a retail store where you can purchase glass art supplies, tools, and unique glass art pieces created by local artists.

Studio Rentals: If you're an experienced glass artist, you may have the option to rent studio space and equipment for your own projects.

Gallery Shop: The gallery shop features a curated selection of glass art and other craft items for sale, making it a great place to find unique gifts or collectibles.

Community Engagement: The Pittsburgh Glass Center is deeply engaged with the local community and often collaborates with schools, artists, and organizations to promote the art of glassmaking.

Special Events: The center hosts special events, openings, and receptions to celebrate new exhibitions and foster a sense of community among art lovers.

Before your visit, check the Pittsburgh Glass Center's official website or local event listings for information on hours of operation, current exhibitions, class schedules, and any special events or workshops that may be taking place. Whether you're a glass art enthusiast, an aspiring artist, or someone looking for a creative and visually engaging experience, the Pittsburgh Glass Center offers a dynamic and hands-on journey into the world of glass art and craftsmanship.

You may come across markers, interpretive signs, and attractions related to the region's history.

Recreational Opportunities: The trail is multi-use, catering to walkers, runners, cyclists, and even equestrians in some sections. It provides a safe and enjoyable environment for physical activity and exploration.

Mileage Options: The trail offers different mileage options, allowing you to customize your adventure. You can choose to tackle shorter sections for a leisurely outing or challenge yourself with a longer trek.

Picnic Areas: Along the route, you may encounter designated picnic areas where you can take a break, enjoy a meal, and soak in the beautiful surroundings.

Wildlife Viewing: The trail's natural setting provides opportunities for observing wildlife, including birds, small mammals, and perhaps even deer or other native creatures.

Water Features: Depending on the section of the trail you explore, you may encounter water features such as creeks, streams, and ponds. These areas offer tranquil spots for reflection and nature appreciation.

Community Events: The trail is occasionally used for community events, races, and outdoor programs. Check local event listings for any upcoming activities or group outings.

Accessible Trails: Some sections of the trail are designed to be accessible for individuals with mobility challenges, making it inclusive for a wide range of visitors.

Biking Opportunities: Cyclists can enjoy the trail's paved and well-maintained paths, making it a favorite destination for bike enthusiasts.

Before your visit, check the Westmoreland Heritage Trail's official website or local information sources for details on trailheads, parking options, current conditions, and any specific guidelines or trail regulations. Whether you're an outdoor enthusiast, a history buff, or someone seeking a scenic and active escape, the Westmoreland Heritage Trail offers a beautiful and rejuvenating journey through the natural and historical landscapes of Western Pennsylvania.

79.Explore the Wood Street Galleries for contemporary art.

Exploring the Wood Street Galleries in Pittsburgh, Pennsylvania, is an opportunity to immerse yourself in contemporary art in a unique and innovative setting. Here's what you can expect when you visit these galleries:

Wood Street Galleries:

Contemporary Art Exhibitions: Wood Street Galleries regularly host contemporary art exhibitions that feature a wide range of art forms, including visual art, digital art, installations, sculptures, and multimedia pieces. You'll have the chance to experience cutting-edge and thought-provoking artworks.

Diverse Artists: The galleries often showcase the work of both emerging and established contemporary artists, offering a diverse range of artistic perspectives and styles.

Interactive Installations: Some exhibitions may include interactive and multimedia installations that engage the senses and encourage audience participation. These installations can be both visually stunning and intellectually engaging.

New Media and Technology: Wood Street Galleries frequently explore the intersection of art and technology. You may encounter artworks that utilize the latest digital media and technology to create immersive and dynamic experiences.

Exhibition Spaces: The galleries feature well-curated exhibition spaces that provide a conducive environment for appreciating contemporary art. The design and layout of the galleries enhance the viewer's connection with the artwork.

Educational Programs: The galleries may offer educational programs, artist talks, and workshops that provide insights into the creative process and the themes explored in the exhibitions.

Cultural and Conceptual Exploration: The art on display often delves into complex cultural, social, and conceptual themes, challenging viewers to think critically and engage with the art on an intellectual and emotional level.

Community Engagement: Wood Street Galleries is deeply connected to the local arts community and often collaborates with artists, organizations, and schools to promote contemporary art and culture.

Art for Sale: If you're an art collector or enthusiast, you may have the opportunity to purchase some of the artworks on display.

Before your visit, check the Wood Street Galleries' official website or local event listings for information on exhibition schedules, gallery hours, admission fees, and any special events or artist talks that may be taking place. Whether you're an art lover, a contemporary art enthusiast, or someone looking for a stimulating and visually engaging experience, Wood Street Galleries offers a dynamic journey into the world of contemporary art and artistic exploration.

80.Attend a performance by Bricolage Production Company.

Attending a performance by the Bricolage Production Company is an immersive and inventive theatrical experience that challenges conventional storytelling and engages the audience in unique ways. Here's what you can expect when you attend a production by Bricolage:

Bricolage Production Company:

Site-Specific Theater: Bricolage often specializes in site-specific theater, creating productions that take place in unconventional and non-traditional locations. This unique approach transforms the performance space into an integral part of the storytelling.

Immersive Experiences: Bricolage is known for immersive and interactive productions that allow the audience to become an active participant in the narrative. You may find yourself involved in the action or decisions that shape the story.

Multidisciplinary Art: The company frequently integrates various art forms, including theater, dance, music, and technology, to create multi-sensory and dynamic performances.

Original Works: Bricolage often produces original and experimental works that challenge traditional theater norms and explore complex themes and narratives.

Engaging Storytelling: The theater is committed to engaging storytelling that pushes the boundaries of conventional narratives and encourages the audience to think critically and emotionally engage with the performance.

Community Engagement: Bricolage is deeply involved with the local community and often hosts educational programs, workshops, and outreach events that enhance the audience's understanding of the creative process and the themes of the productions.

Collaborations: The company frequently collaborates with local and international artists, designers, and creative teams, resulting in productions that are both innovative and diverse in style and approach.

Special Events: In addition to their regular productions, Bricolage often hosts special events, discussions, and workshops to engage with the community and offer behind-the-scenes insights into their creative process.

Before attending a performance, check Bricolage Production Company's official website or local event listings for information on show schedules, ticket availability, and any special events or immersive experiences that may be taking place. Whether you're a theater enthusiast, an advocate for innovative art, or someone seeking a dynamic and unconventional theatrical experience, Bricolage Production Company offers a thought-provoking and immersive journey into the world of experimental theater and storytelling.

81.Take a scenic drive through Raccoon Creek State Park (near Pittsburgh).

Taking a scenic drive through Raccoon Creek State Park, located near Pittsburgh, Pennsylvania, offers a tranquil and immersive experience in the beauty of nature. Here's what you can expect when you embark on a scenic drive through this picturesque park:

Raccoon Creek State Park:

Spectacular Landscapes: Raccoon Creek State Park encompasses 7,572 acres of natural beauty, featuring lush woodlands, meadows, wetlands, and the pristine

Raccoon Lake. Your drive will take you through a variety of captivating landscapes.

Raccoon Lake: The park surrounds Raccoon Lake, a 101-acre body of water known for its calm and serene ambiance. You may encounter the lake during your drive, offering scenic views and the opportunity for a leisurely lakeside stop.

Scenic Overlooks: The park provides several scenic overlooks that offer breathtaking vistas of the lake, woodlands, and hillsides. These overlooks serve as ideal locations for taking in the views and capturing photographs.

Hiking Trails: While driving through the park, you'll come across trailheads for hiking and walking trails. These trails provide the chance to explore the park on foot, appreciating its natural beauty up close.

Picnic Areas: Raccoon Creek State Park features designated picnic areas where you can stop, enjoy a meal, and absorb the natural surroundings. The sounds of the lake and woods create a peaceful atmosphere.

Wildlife Viewing: Keep an eye out for wildlife such as deer, birds, and various small mammals. The park offers opportunities for wildlife sightings, making it a favorite spot for birdwatchers and nature enthusiasts.

Changing Seasons: The park's beauty changes with the seasons. In the spring, wildflowers bloom, while in the fall, the foliage turns vibrant shades of red and orange. Each season provides a unique and picturesque experience.

Boating and Fishing: If you're interested in boating or fishing, Raccoon Creek State Park offers opportunities for these activities. The park has a boat launch and is known for fishing on the lake.

Outdoor Recreation: Depending on the season and park regulations, you might enjoy outdoor activities like hiking, biking, birdwatching, and cross-country skiing during the winter months.

Before your scenic drive, it's a good idea to check the Raccoon Creek State Park's official website or local information sources for details on road conditions, trail access, seasonal activities, and any specific park rules or guidelines that may be in place. Whether you're a nature enthusiast, a lover of the outdoors, or someone seeking a peaceful escape, Raccoon Creek State Park offers a rejuvenating and captivating journey through the natural beauty of Western Pennsylvania.

82. Visit the Harmony Museum (in Harmony, near Pittsburgh).

Visiting the Harmony Museum in Harmony, Pennsylvania, near Pittsburgh, provides a unique opportunity to explore the history of a historic communal settlement. Here's what you can expect when you visit this museum:

Harmony Museum:

Historical Significance: The Harmony Museum is dedicated to preserving the history and heritage of Harmony, Pennsylvania, which was originally founded as a communal settlement by the Harmony Society in the early 19th century. The museum provides insights into the society's religious beliefs, way of life, and its role in the history of Western Pennsylvania.

Exhibitions: The museum features a variety of exhibitions that highlight the history of the Harmony Society and the local region. You can expect to see artifacts, documents, and displays related to the society's communal living, religious practices, and contributions to the community.

Historic Structures: In addition to the museum itself, the Harmony area boasts several well-preserved historic buildings, including the Mennonite Meetinghouse and the Harmonist Barn. You can explore these structures and learn about their history.

Educational Programs: The museum offers educational programs, lectures, and guided tours that delve into the history of the Harmony Society and its impact on the region.

Gift Shop: The museum's gift shop often sells unique items, books, and memorabilia related to the history of Harmony and the Harmony Society.

Community Events: The museum hosts community events and special programs throughout the year, allowing you to engage with the local community and gain a deeper appreciation for the region's history.

Gardens: Harmony features beautifully maintained gardens, which you can explore and enjoy during your visit. These gardens add to the historic ambiance of the town.

Before your visit, check the Harmony Museum's official website or contact them for information on museum hours, admission fees, current exhibitions, and any special events or programs that may be taking place. Whether you're a history enthusiast, a cultural explorer, or someone seeking to understand the unique history of communal societies, the Harmony Museum offers an insightful and engaging journey into the past of Western Pennsylvania and the Harmony Society.

83.Explore the Pittsburgh Playwrights Theatre Company.

Exploring the Pittsburgh Playwrights Theatre Company offers a rich and diverse experience in the world of theater and storytelling. Here's what you can expect when you visit or engage with the Pittsburgh Playwrights Theatre Company:

Pittsburgh Playwrights Theatre Company:

Theatrical Productions: Pittsburgh Playwrights Theatre Company is dedicated to producing a wide range of theatrical productions, including plays, staged readings, and original works. The company often emphasizes contemporary and thought-provoking stories that tackle complex themes and issues.

Diverse Voices: The company places a strong emphasis on presenting the work of local and underrepresented playwrights, as well as celebrating diverse voices and perspectives in the world of theater.

Community Engagement: Pittsburgh Playwrights Theatre Company is deeply connected to the local community and often collaborates with schools, artists, and cultural organizations to promote theater and artistic expression in the region.

Educational Programs: The theater company frequently offers educational programs, workshops, and playwriting opportunities that enhance your understanding of the creative process and theater arts.

Original Works: You can expect to encounter original plays and performances that challenge conventional norms and encourage critical thinking and emotional engagement.

Cultural Enrichment: By attending productions by Pittsburgh Playwrights Theatre Company, you contribute to the cultural vibrancy of the region and support the local arts scene.

Engaging Storytelling: The company is committed to engaging storytelling that explores complex narratives and social issues, providing audiences with thought-provoking and emotionally charged experiences.

Special Events: The theater often hosts special events, opening nights, discussions with the cast and creative team, and community discussions to foster a sense of community among theater enthusiasts.

Before attending a performance, check the Pittsburgh Playwrights Theatre Company's official website or local event listings for information on show schedules, ticket availability, and any special events, workshops, or educational programs that may be taking place. Whether you're a theater aficionado, a supporter of diverse voices in the arts, or someone looking for a stimulating and emotionally engaging theatrical experience, the Pittsburgh Playwrights Theatre Company offers a dynamic journey into the world of contemporary theater and storytelling.

84.Attend a performance by The Pillow Project.

Attending a performance by The Pillow Project is an opportunity to experience avant-garde and immersive contemporary dance and performance art. Here's what you can expect when you attend a production by The Pillow Project:

The Pillow Project:

Experimental Dance: The Pillow Project is known for pushing the boundaries of contemporary dance and performance art. Their productions often feature experimental movements, choreography, and artistic expressions.

Travel to Pittsburgh Pennsylvania

Immersive Performances: The company frequently creates immersive and multi-sensory performances that engage the audience in unique ways. You may find yourself part of the action or surrounded by the performance, blurring the lines between performers and spectators.

Multidisciplinary Approach: The Pillow Project often integrates various art forms, such as music, visual art, video, and technology, into their performances, creating a multi-dimensional and dynamic experience.

Original Works: You can expect to see original and thought-provoking productions that challenge traditional dance and performance norms and explore complex themes and narratives.

Community Engagement: The Pillow Project is deeply connected to the local arts community and often collaborates with artists, organizations, and schools to promote contemporary dance and artistic expression in the region.

Educational Programs: The company offers educational programs, workshops, and dance classes that provide insights into their creative process and encourage audience participation.

Cultural Enrichment: By attending performances by The Pillow Project, you contribute to the cultural vibrancy of the region and support the local arts scene.

Special Events: The company may host special events, post-show discussions, and receptions to engage with the community and offer behind-the-scenes insights into their creative process.

Before attending a performance, check The Pillow Project's official website or local event listings for information on show schedules, ticket availability, and any special events or workshops that may be taking place. Whether you're a contemporary dance enthusiast, a supporter of experimental art, or someone looking for a unique and immersive artistic experience, The Pillow Project offers a dynamic journey into the world of avant-garde dance and performance art.

85. Take a scenic drive through Linn Run State Park (near Pittsburgh).

Taking a scenic drive through Linn Run State Park, located near Pittsburgh, Pennsylvania, offers a serene and picturesque escape into the natural beauty of the Laurel Highlands. Here's what you can expect when you embark on a scenic drive through this charming state park:

Linn Run State Park:

Spectacular Scenery: Linn Run State Park is renowned for its breathtaking natural landscapes, featuring pristine woodlands, meandering streams, and lush greenery. Your drive will take you through a variety of captivating vistas.

Linn Run: The park is named after Linn Run, a picturesque mountain stream that flows through the area. You'll have the chance to see this clear, babbling creek during your drive, offering opportunities for tranquil stops and photo-taking.

Scenic Overlooks: The park provides several scenic overlooks that offer stunning views of the surrounding woodlands, valleys, and hillsides. These overlooks serve as excellent spots for taking in the natural beauty and capturing photographs.

Hiking Trails: As you drive through the park, you'll come across trailheads for hiking and walking paths, allowing you to explore the area on foot and appreciate its natural beauty up close.

Picnic Areas: Linn Run State Park features designated picnic areas where you can pause, enjoy a meal, and absorb the serene natural surroundings. The sounds of the creek and the woods create a peaceful ambiance.

Wildlife Watching: Keep an eye out for wildlife such as deer, birds, and various small mammals. The park offers opportunities for wildlife sightings, making it a favorite spot for birdwatchers and nature enthusiasts.

Changing Seasons: The park's beauty evolves with the seasons. In spring, wildflowers bloom, while in the fall, the foliage turns vibrant shades of red, orange, and gold. Each season provides a unique and picturesque experience.

Recreational Opportunities: Depending on the season and park regulations, you might enjoy activities like hiking, picnicking, birdwatching, and snowshoeing during the winter months.

Before embarking on your scenic drive, check the Linn Run State Park's official website or local information sources for details on road conditions, trail access, seasonal activities, and any specific park rules or guidelines that may be in place. Whether you're a nature lover, an outdoor enthusiast, or someone seeking a peaceful escape in the Laurel Highlands, Linn Run State Park offers a rejuvenating and captivating journey through the natural beauty of Western Pennsylvania.

86. Visit the Westmoreland County Historical

Visiting the Westmoreland County Historical Society in Greensburg, Pennsylvania, provides a unique opportunity to delve into the rich history of the region. Here's what you can expect when you visit this historical society:

Westmoreland County Historical Society:

Historical Artifacts: The society houses a vast collection of historical artifacts, documents, photographs, and memorabilia related to the history of Westmoreland County. You can explore exhibits and displays that span from the county's early days to more recent history.

Interactive Exhibits: The historical society often features interactive exhibits that allow you to engage with history in a hands-on and immersive way. These exhibits can make the past come alive for visitors of all ages.

Local History: The society focuses on preserving and showcasing the local history of Westmoreland County, including its early settlements, industrial heritage, significant events, and prominent figures.

Historic Buildings: The society may have historic buildings or structures that you can explore, providing insights into the architectural and cultural heritage of the region.

Educational Programs: The historical society offers educational programs, lectures, and guided tours that provide in-depth knowledge of the historical aspects of Westmoreland County.

Research Opportunities: If you're interested in genealogy or conducting historical research, the society often provides access to archives and resources that can aid in your research efforts.

Community Events: The society hosts community events, lectures, workshops, and special programs that celebrate the rich history of the region. These events often attract history enthusiasts and the local community.

Gift Shop: The society's gift shop may sell books, publications, and historical items related to Westmoreland County, allowing you to take a piece of local history home with you.

Before your visit, check the Westmoreland County Historical Society's official website or contact them for information on museum hours, admission fees, current exhibits, and any special events or programs that may be taking place. Whether you're a history buff, a genealogy researcher, or someone seeking to understand the local heritage of Westmoreland County, the historical society offers an informative and engaging journey into the past of this region in Western Pennsylvania.

87.Explore the Andy Warhol Bridge.

Exploring the Andy Warhol Bridge in Pittsburgh, Pennsylvania, offers a unique experience that combines art, history, and urban architecture. Here's what you can expect when you visit this iconic bridge:

Andy Warhol Bridge:

Artistic Inspiration: The bridge is named after the famous pop art artist Andy Warhol, who was born in Pittsburgh. The bridge serves as a tribute to his artistic contributions and is an embodiment of his connection to the city.

Colorful Enhancements: One of the standout features of the Andy Warhol Bridge is its vibrant, colorful paint job. The bridge's surface is adorned with bright and lively colors, creating a visual spectacle that stands out against the backdrop of the city.

Suspension Bridge Design: The Andy Warhol Bridge is a suspension bridge, which is an architectural style that adds to its unique and iconic appearance. The design is reminiscent of the many historic bridges that cross Pittsburgh's three rivers.

Pedestrian-Friendly: The bridge is open to both vehicular and pedestrian traffic. You can walk or bike across the bridge to enjoy the panoramic views of the city, including the nearby Warhol Museum, which is dedicated to Andy Warhol's life and art.

Scenic Views: While on the bridge, you can take in scenic views of the Allegheny River and the surrounding cityscape. The bridge offers fantastic opportunities for capturing photographs of the city's skyline.

Public Art: The bridge's colorful paintwork and dedication to Andy Warhol represent a form of public art, contributing to the cultural landscape of Pittsburgh.

Gateway to North Shore: The Andy Warhol Bridge serves as a gateway to the North Shore of Pittsburgh, which is home to attractions like PNC Park, Heinz Field, and the Carnegie Science Center.

Cultural Significance: This bridge is more than just a transportation route; it symbolizes the city's artistic and cultural identity and showcases its deep appreciation for the arts.

When you visit the Andy Warhol Bridge, consider taking a leisurely stroll or bike ride across it to fully appreciate the artistic and architectural beauty it offers. Additionally, explore the surrounding area to discover the many cultural and recreational attractions that Pittsburgh has to offer.

88.Attend a performance by the Attack Theatre.

Attending a performance by Attack Theatre is an opportunity to immerse yourself in contemporary dance and performance art that's dynamic and thought-provoking. Here's what you can expect when you attend a production by Attack Theatre:

Attack Theatre:

Contemporary Dance: Attack Theatre is known for pushing the boundaries of contemporary dance, often incorporating innovative movement, choreography, and artistic expression into their performances.

Immersive Experiences: The company frequently creates immersive and multi-sensory performances that engage the audience in unique ways. You might find yourself part of the action or surrounded by the performance, blurring the lines between performers and spectators.

Multidisciplinary Approach: Attack Theatre often integrates various art forms, including music, visual art, video, and technology, into their performances. This creates a multi-dimensional and dynamic experience that combines various artistic elements.

Original Works: You can expect to see original and thought-provoking productions that challenge traditional dance norms and encourage critical thinking and emotional engagement.

Community Engagement: Attack Theatre is deeply connected to the local arts community and often collaborates with artists, organizations, and schools to promote contemporary dance and artistic expression in the region.

Educational Programs: The company offers educational programs, workshops, and dance classes that provide insights into their creative process and encourage audience participation.

Cultural Enrichment: By attending performances by Attack Theatre, you contribute to the cultural vibrancy of the region and support the local arts scene.

Special Events: The company often hosts special events, discussions with the cast and creative team, and community receptions to engage with the audience and offer behind-the-scenes insights into their creative process.

Before attending a performance, check Attack Theatre's official website or local event listings for information on show schedules, ticket availability, and any special events, workshops, or educational programs that may be taking place. Whether you're a dance enthusiast, an advocate for contemporary art, or someone looking for a unique and immersive artistic experience, Attack Theatre offers a dynamic journey into the world of avant-garde dance and performance art.

89. Take a scenic drive through Yellow Creek State Park (near Pittsburgh).

Taking a scenic drive through Yellow Creek State Park, located near Pittsburgh, Pennsylvania, offers a tranquil and picturesque escape into the natural beauty of the region. Here's what you can expect when you embark on a scenic drive through this state park:

Yellow Creek State Park:

Spectacular Landscapes: Yellow Creek State Park encompasses 2,981 acres of natural beauty, featuring lush forests, rolling hills, and the 720-acre Yellow Creek Lake. Your drive will take you through a variety of captivating landscapes.

Yellow Creek Lake: The park surrounds Yellow Creek Lake, a serene and picturesque body of water. You may encounter the lake during your drive, offering scenic views and the opportunity for a leisurely lakeside stop.

Scenic Overlooks: The park provides several scenic overlooks that offer breathtaking vistas of the lake, woodlands, and hillsides. These overlooks serve as ideal locations for taking in the views and capturing photographs.

Hiking Trails: While driving through the park, you'll come across trailheads for hiking and walking trails. These trails provide the chance to explore the park on foot, appreciating its natural beauty up close.

Picnic Areas: Yellow Creek State Park features designated picnic areas where you can stop, enjoy a meal, and absorb the natural surroundings. The sounds of the lake and the woods create a peaceful atmosphere.

Wildlife Viewing: Keep an eye out for wildlife such as deer, birds, and various small mammals. The park offers opportunities for wildlife sightings, making it a favorite spot for birdwatchers and nature enthusiasts.

Changing Seasons: The park's beauty changes with the seasons. In the spring, wildflowers bloom, while in the fall, the foliage turns vibrant shades of red, orange, and yellow. Each season provides a unique and picturesque experience.

Recreational Opportunities: Depending on the season and park regulations, you might enjoy outdoor activities like hiking, fishing, boating, and swimming during the summer months.

Before your scenic drive, check Yellow Creek State Park's official website or local information sources for details on road conditions, trail access, seasonal activities, and any specific park rules or guidelines that may be in place. Whether you're a nature lover, an outdoor enthusiast, or someone seeking a peaceful escape in the Pennsylvania countryside, Yellow Creek State Park offers a rejuvenating and captivating journey through the natural beauty of the region.

90. Visit the Allegheny Observatory.

Visiting the Allegheny Observatory in Pittsburgh, Pennsylvania, offers a fascinating opportunity to explore astronomy, scientific research, and the history of this renowned institution. Here's what you can expect when you visit the Allegheny Observatory:

Allegheny Observatory:

Astronomical Research: The Allegheny Observatory is dedicated to astronomical research, making it a hub for the study of celestial objects, including stars, planets, and galaxies. It plays a vital role in advancing our understanding of the universe.

Historical Significance: The observatory has a rich history, dating back to its founding in 1859. It is one of the oldest observatories in the United States and has played a pivotal role in astronomy and astrophysics research.

Telescopes: The observatory houses a collection of telescopes, including the famous Thaw Refractor, which is one of the largest and oldest refracting telescopes in the world. You can expect to see these remarkable instruments up close.

Observation Programs: The observatory often offers public observation programs, allowing visitors to view celestial objects through their telescopes.

These programs provide a unique opportunity to stargaze and learn about the cosmos.

Educational Exhibits: Inside the observatory, you'll find educational exhibits and displays related to astronomy, astrophysics, and the history of the institution. These exhibits help visitors gain a deeper understanding of the universe and the observatory's contributions to science.

Lectures and Workshops: The observatory may host lectures, workshops, and educational programs that engage the public in the wonders of the cosmos and the latest discoveries in the field of astronomy.

Historic Building: The observatory building itself is a historical and architectural gem. Its iconic dome and beautiful surroundings contribute to the overall experience.

Scenic Location: The Allegheny Observatory is situated on a hill overlooking the city of Pittsburgh, providing panoramic views of the city and the night sky.

Before your visit, check the Allegheny Observatory's official website or contact them for information on visiting hours, public programs, admission fees, and any special events or lectures that may be taking place. Whether you're a passionate stargazer, an astronomy enthusiast, or someone simply curious about the cosmos, the Allegheny Observatory offers an enlightening and awe-inspiring journey into the world of astronomy and scientific exploration.

91.Explore the Wood Street Commons for public art installations.

Exploring the Wood Street Commons in Pittsburgh, Pennsylvania, offers an engaging experience with public art installations and cultural enrichment. Here's what you can expect when you visit this dynamic urban space:

Wood Street Commons - Public Art Installations:

Contemporary Art: Wood Street Commons frequently hosts rotating public art installations, including sculptures, murals, and interactive pieces created by local and international artists. You can expect to encounter a diverse range of contemporary artistic expressions.

Interactive Art: Some of the installations may be interactive, encouraging visitors to engage with the artwork. This can create a unique and participatory experience for those exploring the space.

Cultural Enrichment: The public art installations in Wood Street Commons contribute to the cultural vibrancy of Pittsburgh and reflect the city's commitment to showcasing art in public spaces. It's a place where art and culture converge.

Changing Exhibits: As the exhibits change periodically, you can enjoy different artistic expressions and experiences with each visit. This keeps the space fresh and continuously evolving.

Photographic Opportunities: The public art installations often provide fantastic backdrops for photography, allowing you to capture memorable moments and share them with others.

Community Engagement: Wood Street Commons serves as a hub for community engagement, often hosting events and activities related to the arts. These events can foster a sense of connection and appreciation for the local art scene.

Art Appreciation: Whether you're a dedicated art enthusiast or someone who simply enjoys art in public spaces, Wood Street Commons offers a space for art appreciation that's easily accessible and open to all.

Before your visit, check for information about the current public art installations and any events that may be taking place in Wood Street Commons. Whether you're a local resident or a visitor to Pittsburgh, exploring this urban space with its public art installations is a great way to engage with the city's cultural scene and appreciate the creativity of artists in the region.

92.Attend a performance by the No Name Players.

Attending a performance by the No Name Players is an opportunity to experience innovative and thought-provoking theater productions. Here's what you can expect when you attend a show by the No Name Players:

Travel to Pittsburgh Pennsylvania

No Name Players:

Contemporary Theater: No Name Players are known for their contemporary and often edgy approach to theater. Their productions tackle a wide range of themes, from modern societal issues to personal narratives.

Emerging Artists: The company often features emerging artists, playwrights, and directors, providing a platform for new voices in the theater world.

Original Works: You can expect to see original and unique productions, including plays, performance art, and other forms of experimental theater. These works challenge traditional norms and invite critical thinking.

Intimate Settings: No Name Players often choose intimate venues for their performances, creating an up-close and personal atmosphere that allows for a more immersive experience.

Community Engagement: The company is deeply connected to the local arts community and often collaborates with artists, organizations, and schools to promote contemporary theater and artistic expression in the region.

Educational Programs: No Name Players offer educational programs, workshops, and opportunities for aspiring actors and theater enthusiasts to engage with the creative process.

Cultural Enrichment: By attending performances by No Name Players, you contribute to the cultural vibrancy of the region and support the local arts scene.

Special Events: The company may host special events, post-show discussions, and community receptions to engage with the audience and offer behind-the-scenes insights into their creative process.

Before attending a performance, check the No Name Players' official website or local event listings for information on show schedules, ticket availability, and any special events or workshops that may be taking place. Whether you're a theater enthusiast, an advocate for contemporary art, or someone looking for unique and intellectually stimulating theatrical experiences, No Name Players offer a dynamic journey into the world of innovative and experimental theater.

93. Take a scenic drive through Keystone State Park (near Pittsburgh).

Taking a scenic drive through Keystone State Park, located near Pittsburgh, Pennsylvania, offers a peaceful and picturesque journey through nature. Here's what you can expect when you embark on a scenic drive through this state park:

Keystone State Park:

Natural Beauty: Keystone State Park encompasses 1,200 acres of pristine woodlands, rolling hills, and a 78-acre lake. Your drive will take you through the heart of this natural beauty.

Keystone Lake: The park surrounds Keystone Lake, a serene and picturesque body of water. You may come across the lake during your drive, providing opportunities for lakeside stops and enjoying the view.

Scenic Overlooks: The park provides several scenic overlooks that offer stunning views of the lake, woodlands, and hillsides. These overlooks serve as excellent spots for taking in the natural beauty and capturing photographs.

Hiking Trails: While driving through the park, you'll come across trailheads for hiking and walking paths, allowing you to explore the area on foot and appreciate its natural beauty up close.

Picnic Areas: Keystone State Park features designated picnic areas where you can pause, enjoy a meal, and take in the serene natural surroundings. The sounds of the lake and the woods create a tranquil atmosphere.

Wildlife Watching: Keep an eye out for wildlife such as deer, birds, and various small mammals. The park offers opportunities for wildlife sightings, making it a favorite spot for birdwatchers and nature enthusiasts.

Changing Seasons: The park's beauty evolves with the seasons. In spring, wildflowers bloom, while in the fall, the foliage turns vibrant shades of red, orange, and yellow. Each season provides a unique and picturesque experience.

Recreational Opportunities: Depending on the season and park regulations, you might enjoy activities like hiking, fishing, boating, swimming, and camping during the summer months.

Before embarking on your scenic drive, check Keystone State Park's official website or local information sources for details on road conditions, trail access, seasonal activities, and any specific park rules or guidelines that may be in place. Whether you're a nature enthusiast, an outdoor lover, or someone seeking a peaceful escape in the Pennsylvania countryside, Keystone State Park offers a rejuvenating and captivating journey through the natural beauty of the region.

94. Visit the Soldiers & Sailors Memorial Hall Museum.

Visiting the Soldiers & Sailors Memorial Hall Museum in Pittsburgh, Pennsylvania, offers a profound and educational experience that honors the contributions of the men and women who served in the United States military. Here's what you can expect when you visit this historic institution:

Soldiers & Sailors Memorial Hall Museum:

Military History: The museum is dedicated to preserving and showcasing the military history of the United States, with a particular focus on the contributions and sacrifices of veterans from Western Pennsylvania. It features a vast collection of artifacts, documents, and memorabilia.

Historical Exhibits: The museum houses a wide range of exhibits that provide insights into the various conflicts in which American soldiers and sailors have served. You can explore exhibits dedicated to World War I, World War II, the Korean War, the Vietnam War, and more.

Artifacts: You'll encounter an array of military artifacts, including uniforms, weapons, equipment, and personal items that offer a tangible connection to the experiences of service members throughout history.

Veteran Stories: The museum often features personal accounts and stories of local veterans who served in different branches of the military. These narratives provide a human perspective on the challenges and triumphs of military service.

Educational Programs: The museum offers educational programs, lectures, and guided tours that provide a deeper understanding of military history and the sacrifices made by veterans.

Memorial Hall: The architecture of the building itself is impressive and serves as a memorial to honor the men and women who have served in the military. The grand Memorial Hall features sculptures and plaques commemorating the fallen.

Community Engagement: The museum hosts community events, lectures, workshops, and special programs related to military history and the experiences of veterans. These events often attract history enthusiasts, veterans, and the local community.

Gift Shop: The museum's gift shop may offer books, publications, and military-related items, allowing you to take a piece of military history home with you.

Before your visit, check the Soldiers & Sailors Memorial Hall Museum's official website or contact them for information on museum hours, admission fees, current exhibits, and any special events or programs that may be taking place. Whether you're a history buff, a military enthusiast, or someone seeking to pay tribute to the nation's veterans, the Soldiers & Sailors Memorial Hall Museum offers an enlightening and poignant journey into the history and sacrifices of American service members.

95.Explore the USS Requin, a historic submarine museum.

Exploring the USS Requin, a historic submarine museum located in Pittsburgh, Pennsylvania, offers a unique opportunity to step back in time and experience the life and operations of a Cold War-era submarine. Here's what you can expect when you visit the USS Requin:

USS Requin Submarine Museum:

Historical Submarine: The USS Requin (SS-481) is a Tench-class submarine that served in the United States Navy from 1945 to 1971. It was initially constructed during the final stages of World War II and later played a significant role during the Cold War.

Guided Tours: When you visit the USS Requin, you can expect a guided tour of the submarine. Knowledgeable guides will take you through the sub's compartments and explain its history, operations, and the experiences of the crew.

Authentic Interior: The interior of the USS Requin has been preserved to resemble its original condition during the Cold War era. You can explore the control room, crew quarters, engine room, and other areas, getting a sense of what life was like for submariners during this period.

Historical Exhibits: In addition to the submarine itself, the museum often features exhibits and displays that provide context about the Cold War, naval history, and the role of submarines in defense and warfare.

Educational Programs: The museum offers educational programs and activities that engage visitors in learning about naval history, technology, and the experiences of submariners.

Scenic Views: The USS Requin is moored on the Ohio River, and you can enjoy scenic views of the river and the surrounding area from the submarine.

Family-Friendly: The museum is suitable for visitors of all ages, making it an educational and entertaining outing for families.

Community Engagement: The USS Requin Submarine Museum often hosts special events, lectures, and community programs related to naval history, veterans, and the role of submarines in the Cold War.

Before your visit, check the USS Requin Submarine Museum's official website or contact them for information on museum hours, admission fees, guided tour schedules, and any special events or programs that may be taking place. Whether you're a history enthusiast, a naval history buff, or someone simply curious about life aboard a submarine, exploring the USS Requin offers an immersive and enlightening journey into the history of naval technology and military service during the Cold War.

96.Attend a performance by the Jewish Theatre of Pittsburgh.

Attending a performance by the Jewish Theatre of Pittsburgh offers a unique opportunity to engage with thought-provoking and culturally significant theatrical productions. Here's what you can expect when you attend a show by the Jewish Theatre of Pittsburgh:

Jewish Theatre of Pittsburgh:

Cultural Significance: The Jewish Theatre of Pittsburgh often presents plays and performances that explore Jewish themes, traditions, and experiences. These productions contribute to the cultural enrichment of the community and celebrate the diverse facets of Jewish identity.

Theatrical Excellence: The company is dedicated to delivering high-quality theatrical productions, with a focus on engaging storytelling, talented actors, and creative direction.

Diverse Themes: While some productions may focus on Jewish history, heritage, and contemporary Jewish life, others explore universal themes that resonate with audiences from all backgrounds. The theater offers a rich tapestry of stories and experiences.

Educational and Outreach Programs: The Jewish Theatre of Pittsburgh may offer educational programs, discussions, and community outreach activities that provide a deeper understanding of the themes explored in their productions.

Cultural Engagement: By attending performances by the Jewish Theatre of Pittsburgh, you can engage with the cultural and artistic vibrancy of the local Jewish community and gain insights into Jewish traditions, history, and contemporary life.

Community Events: The company often hosts events, post-show discussions, and receptions that encourage audience interaction and provide an opportunity to connect with fellow theater enthusiasts and the creative team.

Before attending a performance, check the Jewish Theatre of Pittsburgh's official website or local event listings for information on show schedules, ticket availability, and any special events or workshops that may be taking place. Whether you're a theater enthusiast, interested in Jewish culture, or someone seeking engaging and culturally significant productions, the Jewish Theatre of Pittsburgh offers a dynamic journey into the world of theater and cultural exploration.

97.Take a scenic drive through Oil Creek State Park (near Pittsburgh).

Taking a scenic drive through Oil Creek State Park, which is located approximately 90 miles north of Pittsburgh, offers a serene and picturesque journey through the beautiful natural landscapes of Pennsylvania. Here's what you can expect when you embark on a scenic drive through this state park:

Oil Creek State Park:

Natural Beauty: Oil Creek State Park covers over 7,000 acres and is known for its stunning natural beauty. The park is situated in the heart of the Pennsylvania Oil Region, offering landscapes of forests, hills, and the winding Oil Creek.

Historic Significance: The park holds historical importance as it was the site of the world's first commercial oil well, known as the Drake Well, which was drilled in 1859. You may pass by historical markers and exhibits related to the oil industry.

Scenic Drives: There are well-maintained roads and scenic byways within the park that allow you to take in the picturesque surroundings from the comfort of your vehicle. These drives offer views of woodlands, the creek, and historical sites.

Hiking Trails: While driving, you might notice trailheads leading to hiking and walking paths. These trails provide opportunities for closer exploration, with some leading to overlooks and points of interest.

Picnic Areas: The park features designated picnic areas where you can take a break, enjoy a meal, and soak in the natural surroundings. The babbling creek and lush forests create a tranquil atmosphere.

Wildlife Viewing: Keep an eye out for wildlife such as deer, birds, and other animals that call the park home. Oil Creek State Park is a favorite spot for birdwatchers and nature enthusiasts.

Changing Seasons: The park's beauty evolves with the seasons. In spring, wildflowers bloom, while autumn brings vibrant foliage and breathtaking colors. Each season offers a unique and memorable experience.

Recreational Opportunities: Depending on the season and park regulations, you might engage in outdoor activities like hiking, fishing, boating, and wildlife observation. The park offers a variety of recreational opportunities.

Before starting your scenic drive, check the official Oil Creek State Park website or contact the park office for information on road conditions, trail access, seasonal activities, and any specific park rules or guidelines. Whether you're a nature lover, an outdoor enthusiast, or someone seeking a peaceful escape in the Pennsylvania countryside, a scenic drive through Oil Creek State Park provides a rejuvenating and captivating journey through the natural beauty of the region.

98. Visit the Penn Brewery for traditional German beer and cuisine.

Visiting the Penn Brewery in Pittsburgh, Pennsylvania, provides an opportunity to savor traditional German beer and cuisine in an authentic and welcoming atmosphere. Here's what you can expect when you visit the Penn Brewery:

Penn Brewery:

Traditional German Beer: Penn Brewery is renowned for its commitment to brewing authentic German-style beer. You can expect to find a variety of classic German beer styles, including lagers, pilsners, bocks, and wheat beers. Their beer selection is brewed using traditional German methods and adheres to the Reinheitsgebot (German Beer Purity Law).

Biergarten: The brewery often features a charming outdoor Biergarten (beer garden) where you can enjoy your beer al fresco during the warmer months. It's an excellent spot to soak in the atmosphere and enjoy the company of friends and fellow beer enthusiasts.

German Cuisine: Penn Brewery offers a menu that includes a range of traditional German dishes, such as schnitzel, sausages, sauerkraut, pretzels, and strudel. The cuisine is prepared with an emphasis on authenticity, so you can savor the flavors of Germany.

Live Music: The brewery may host live music events and entertainment, especially during special occasions or festivals. This adds to the festive and convivial ambiance.

CLI

Cultural Events: Penn Brewery often celebrates German cultural events and holidays, such as Oktoberfest, where you can experience the customs and traditions of Germany.

Tours: The brewery may offer guided tours that provide insights into the beer-making process, the brewery's history, and the cultural significance of German beer and cuisine.

Retail Shop: You can purchase Penn Brewery's beer and merchandise, including branded glassware and clothing, so you can take a piece of the experience home with you.

Before your visit, check the Penn Brewery's official website for information on hours of operation, menus, special events, and any guided tours that may be available. Whether you're a beer enthusiast, a lover of German food, or someone seeking a unique and culturally rich dining experience, the Penn Brewery offers a delightful journey into the world of traditional German beer, cuisine, and hospitality.

99.Explore the Soldiers & Sailors Memorial Hall & Museum.

Exploring the Soldiers & Sailors Memorial Hall & Museum in Pittsburgh, Pennsylvania, offers a deep and educational experience dedicated to honoring the sacrifices and contributions of military veterans. Here's what you can expect when you visit this historic institution:

Soldiers & Sailors Memorial Hall & Museum:

Military History: The Soldiers & Sailors Memorial Hall & Museum is dedicated to preserving and showcasing the military history of the United States, with a particular focus on the contributions and sacrifices of veterans from Western Pennsylvania. It features a vast collection of artifacts, documents, and memorabilia.

Historical Exhibits: The museum houses a wide range of exhibits that provide insights into the various conflicts in which American soldiers and sailors have served. You can explore exhibits dedicated to World War I, World War II, the Korean War, the Vietnam War, and more.

Artifacts: You'll encounter an array of military artifacts, including uniforms, weapons, equipment, and personal items that offer a tangible connection to the experiences of service members throughout history.

Veteran Stories: The museum often features personal accounts and stories of local veterans who served in different branches of the military. These narratives provide a human perspective on the challenges and triumphs of military service.

Educational Programs: The museum offers educational programs, lectures, and guided tours that provide a deeper understanding of military history and the sacrifices made by veterans.

Memorial Hall: The architecture of the building itself is impressive and serves as a memorial to honor the men and women who have served in the military. The grand Memorial Hall features sculptures and plaques commemorating the fallen.

Community Engagement: The museum hosts community events, lectures, workshops, and special programs related to military history, veterans, and the role of soldiers and sailors in the defense of the nation.

Gift Shop: The museum's gift shop may offer books, publications, and military-related items, allowing you to take a piece of military history home with you.

Before your visit, check the Soldiers & Sailors Memorial Hall & Museum's official website or contact them for information on museum hours, admission fees, current exhibits, and any special events or programs that may be taking place. Whether you're a history buff, a military enthusiast, or someone seeking to pay tribute to the nation's veterans, the Soldiers & Sailors Memorial Hall & Museum offers an enlightening and poignant journey into the history and sacrifices of American service members.

100.Attend a performance by the Attack Theatre.

Attending a performance by the Attack Theatre in Pittsburgh, Pennsylvania, offers an immersive and artistic experience, as this contemporary dance company is known for its innovative and boundary-pushing performances. Here's what you can expect when you attend a show by the Attack Theatre:

Attack Theatre:

Contemporary Dance: Attack Theatre specializes in contemporary dance, which often combines elements of modern dance, ballet, and other movement forms to create visually stunning and emotionally resonant performances.

Experimental and Collaborative: The company is known for its experimental and collaborative approach to dance, often working with artists from various disciplines, such as musicians, visual artists, and multimedia creators. This results in performances that are both visually and sonically captivating.

Engaging Storytelling: Attack Theatre's productions often feature compelling narratives, themes, and storytelling through movement. These performances can be thought-provoking and emotionally evocative.

Interactive Elements: Some shows may incorporate interactive elements, engaging the audience in the performance and creating a unique and participatory experience.

Community Engagement: Attack Theatre is deeply connected to the local arts community and often hosts educational programs, workshops, and community engagement activities, offering opportunities for individuals to explore dance and the creative process.

Special Events: The company may host special events, post-show discussions, and community receptions that allow audience members to engage with the dancers and artistic team.

Before attending a performance, check the Attack Theatre's official website or local event listings for information on show schedules, ticket availability, and any special events or workshops that may be taking place. Whether you're a dance enthusiast, an advocate for contemporary art, or someone looking for unique and intellectually stimulating artistic experiences, Attack Theatre offers a dynamic journey into the world of innovative and experimental dance.

101.Take a scenic drive through Opossum Lake (near Pittsburgh).

Taking a scenic drive through Opossum Lake, located near Pittsburgh, Pennsylvania, offers a peaceful and picturesque journey through the natural beauty of the region. Here's what you can expect when you embark on a scenic drive around Opossum Lake:

Opossum Lake:

Natural Beauty: Opossum Lake is a serene and picturesque lake surrounded by lush forests and rolling hills. As you drive along the lake's perimeter, you'll be treated to scenic views of the water and the pristine countryside.

Scenic Route: There may be designated roads or routes that take you around the lake, providing opportunities to enjoy the tranquil surroundings from the comfort of your vehicle.

Picnic Spots: The lake area often features designated picnic areas where you can stop for a break and enjoy a meal while taking in the beauty of the natural surroundings.

Wildlife Watching: Keep an eye out for wildlife such as birds, waterfowl, and possibly deer or other animals that inhabit the area. Opossum Lake and its surroundings are often visited by birdwatchers and nature enthusiasts.

Fishing: If you're a fishing enthusiast, the lake offers opportunities for angling. Check local regulations and bring your fishing gear if you wish to cast a line during your visit.

Seasonal Changes: Opossum Lake's beauty varies with the seasons. In spring, you'll see wildflowers in bloom, while autumn brings vibrant foliage. Each season provides a unique and memorable experience.

Recreational Opportunities: Depending on the season and park regulations, you might engage in outdoor activities like hiking, nature walks, and wildlife observation.

Before your scenic drive, check for information on the condition of the roads, access points, and any seasonal activities that may be taking place around Opossum Lake. Whether you're a nature enthusiast, an outdoor lover, or someone seeking a tranquil escape into the natural beauty of the Pennsylvania countryside, a scenic drive around Opossum Lake offers a rejuvenating and captivating journey through the region's pristine landscapes.

102. Visit the August Wilson Center for African American Culture.

Visiting the August Wilson Center for African American Culture in Pittsburgh, Pennsylvania, offers an enriching and cultural experience celebrating the contributions of African Americans to the arts, culture, and history. Here's what you can expect when you visit the August Wilson Center:

August Wilson Center for African American Culture:

Cultural Exhibits: The center often hosts rotating exhibits and showcases dedicated to African American art, history, and culture. These exhibits may include visual art, photography, sculpture, and other forms of artistic expression.

August Wilson's Legacy: The center honors the legacy of August Wilson, the renowned playwright, and Pittsburgh native known for his powerful portrayals of the African American experience. You can explore exhibits and materials related to his life and work.

Performing Arts: The center may feature live performances, including music, dance, theater, and spoken word events, often highlighting the talents of African American artists and performers.

Educational Programs: The August Wilson Center offers educational programs, workshops, lectures, and discussions that provide insights into African American history, art, and culture. These programs often engage visitors in meaningful and thought-provoking conversations.

Community Engagement: The center often hosts community events, forums, and activities designed to promote cultural exchange, unity, and understanding. These events may be open to the public and encourage interaction with artists and thought leaders.

Gift Shop: You can find a gift shop that offers books, publications, art, and merchandise related to African American culture, allowing you to take a piece of the experience home with you.

Special Events: Throughout the year, the center hosts special events, celebrations, and festivals that commemorate important moments in African American history and culture.

Before your visit, check the August Wilson Center's official website or contact them for information on current exhibits, hours of operation, admission fees, and any special events or programs that may be taking place. Whether you're an art enthusiast, a history buff, or someone interested in exploring the diverse and rich culture of African Americans, the August Wilson Center for African American Culture offers a dynamic journey into the world of African American art and heritage.

103.Explore the Wood Street T Station for its art installations.

Exploring the Wood Street T Station in Pittsburgh, Pennsylvania, for its art installations provides a unique and creative experience in the heart of the city. Here's what you can expect when you visit the Wood Street T Station:

Wood Street T Station Art Installations:

Public Art: The Wood Street T Station is renowned for its public art installations, which are integrated into the station's design and architecture. You'll encounter a variety of artworks that contribute to the station's vibrant atmosphere.

Contemporary Art: The art at the station often reflects contemporary trends and showcases the work of local and international artists. These installations may include sculptures, murals, digital art, and other forms of creative expression.

Rotating Exhibits: The station may feature rotating exhibits, ensuring that there's always something new and fresh to see when you visit. This dynamic approach to art keeps the space engaging and ever-changing.

Local Flavor: Some art installations at Wood Street T Station may capture the essence of Pittsburgh and its culture, offering a unique blend of creativity and local identity.

Passenger Engagement: The art installations create an engaging environment for passengers and visitors, providing a visual feast that can be enjoyed while waiting for public transportation.

Photographic Opportunities: The station's art provides an excellent backdrop for photography. Whether you're an art enthusiast or simply looking for a unique Instagram-worthy spot, the Wood Street T Station has you covered.

Before visiting, you can check the Port Authority of Allegheny County's official website or local information sources for details on the art installations currently on display at the Wood Street T Station. Whether you're an art aficionado, a commuter, or someone interested in public art, the station offers an imaginative and visually appealing journey into the world of contemporary art.

104.Attend a performance by Pittsburgh Musical Theater.

Attending a performance by Pittsburgh Musical Theater offers an exciting and immersive theatrical experience in Pittsburgh, Pennsylvania. Here's what you can expect when you attend a show by Pittsburgh Musical Theater:

Pittsburgh Musical Theater:

Broad Range of Shows: Pittsburgh Musical Theater produces a diverse selection of musicals, from classic Broadway hits to contemporary productions. You can enjoy performances of beloved musicals, as well as lesser-known gems.

Talented Cast: The company features talented and passionate performers who bring the characters and stories to life with exceptional singing, acting, and dancing.

High-Quality Productions: Pittsburgh Musical Theater is known for its commitment to high-quality productions. The performances often include professional-level staging, costumes, lighting, and set design.

Family-Friendly: Many of the shows are family-friendly, making them suitable for audiences of all ages. It's a great way to introduce children to the magic of live theater.

Musical Variety: Whether you enjoy the catchy tunes of classic musicals or prefer modern, rock-infused productions, Pittsburgh Musical Theater offers a wide range of musical styles to suit various tastes.

Educational Programs: The theater company often engages with the local community and offers educational programs, including youth and adult classes, workshops, and special events that encourage participation in the arts.

Community Engagement: You can often engage with the artistic community by attending post-show discussions, special events, and social gatherings with the cast and crew.

Before attending a performance, check the Pittsburgh Musical Theater's official website or local event listings for information on show schedules, ticket availability, and any special events or workshops that may be taking place. Whether you're a theater enthusiast, a lover of musicals, or someone looking for a memorable and entertaining night out, Pittsburgh Musical Theater provides a dynamic journey into the world of musical theater and performing arts.

105.Take a scenic drive through Lake Arthur (near Pittsburgh).

Taking a scenic drive through Lake Arthur, located within Moraine State Park near Pittsburgh, Pennsylvania, offers a tranquil and picturesque journey through the beautiful natural landscapes of the region. Here's what you can expect when you embark on a scenic drive around Lake Arthur:

Natural Beauty: Lake Arthur is a serene and expansive reservoir surrounded by lush forests and rolling hills. The drive around the lake provides you with picturesque views of the water and the pristine countryside.

Scenic Route: The park often features designated roads or routes that take you around the lake, providing opportunities to enjoy the tranquil surroundings from the comfort of your vehicle.

Picnic Spots: You may find designated picnic areas along the route where you can stop for a break, enjoy a meal, and take in the beauty of the natural surroundings. The sound of the water and the serene environment make for an excellent picnic spot.

Wildlife Watching: Keep an eye out for wildlife such as birds, waterfowl, and other animals that call the area home. Lake Arthur and its surroundings are a popular destination for birdwatchers and nature enthusiasts.

Boating: If you're a boating enthusiast, Lake Arthur offers opportunities for water recreation. You may see sailboats, canoes, and kayaks on the water, providing an additional layer of natural beauty.

Recreational Opportunities: Depending on the season and park regulations, you might engage in outdoor activities such as hiking, fishing, boating, and wildlife observation. The park offers a variety of recreational opportunities.

Before starting your scenic drive, check the Moraine State Park's official website or contact the park office for information on road conditions, trail access, seasonal activities, and any specific park rules or guidelines. Whether you're a nature lover, an outdoor enthusiast, or someone seeking a tranquil escape into the natural beauty of the Pennsylvania countryside, a scenic drive around Lake Arthur offers a rejuvenating and captivating journey through the region's pristine landscapes.

106. Visit the Andy Warhol Museum.

Visiting the Andy Warhol Museum in Pittsburgh, Pennsylvania, is a must for art enthusiasts and fans of the iconic pop artist Andy Warhol. Here's what you can expect when you visit the Andy Warhol Museum:

Andy Warhol Museum:

Andy Warhol's Legacy: The museum is dedicated to preserving and celebrating the life, work, and legacy of Andy Warhol, one of the most influential artists of the 20th century. You can explore the world of this enigmatic artist through his art, personal artifacts, and archives.

Extensive Collection: The museum houses an extensive collection of Warhol's artworks, including his iconic pop art pieces, silkscreens, paintings, and photographs. You'll have the opportunity to see some of his most famous works up close.

Rotating Exhibits: In addition to its permanent collection, the museum often hosts rotating exhibits that explore various aspects of Warhol's work, life, and influence on contemporary art and culture.

Interactive Experiences: Some exhibits feature interactive elements, allowing visitors to engage with Warhol's artistic techniques and experiment with screen printing and other art forms.

Artifacts and Archives: You'll find an array of Warhol's personal artifacts, such as clothing, letters, and personal memorabilia. The museum also houses Warhol's Time Capsules, a unique collection of his personal archives.

Educational Programs: The museum offers educational programs, lectures, workshops, and guided tours that provide insights into Warhol's art, creative process, and his impact on the art world.

Pop Culture and Beyond: The museum often explores Warhol's influence on pop culture, fashion, music, and more. You can gain a deeper understanding of how his work has permeated various aspects of society.

Gift Shop: The museum's gift shop offers books, publications, art prints, and Warhol-inspired merchandise, allowing you to take home a piece of the Warhol experience.

Before your visit, check the Andy Warhol Museum's official website for information on hours of operation, admission fees, current exhibits, and any special events or programs that may be taking place. Whether you're an art aficionado, a Warhol enthusiast, or someone seeking to explore the intersection of art and popular culture, the Andy Warhol Museum offers a dynamic journey into the world of this iconic artist.

107.Explore the Nationality Rooms at the University of Pittsburgh.

Exploring the Nationality Rooms at the University of Pittsburgh is like embarking on a cultural journey around the world without leaving the city. Here's what you can expect when you visit the Nationality Rooms:

Nationality Rooms at the University of Pittsburgh:

Cultural Diversity: The Nationality Rooms represent a diverse range of cultures from around the world. Each room is designed to reflect the cultural heritage, history, and traditions of a specific nationality or ethnic group.

Architectural Diversity: What makes the Nationality Rooms unique is that each room is designed in the architectural style of the respective country. As you move from room to room, you'll notice striking differences in design, decor, and ambiance.

Educational Experience: The Nationality Rooms serve as active classrooms for the University of Pittsburgh, so you might find students and professors engaged in lectures and classes. This creates a dynamic and educational environment.

Guided Tours: The University of Pittsburgh often offers guided tours of the Nationality Rooms. Knowledgeable guides provide historical and cultural insights about each room, making your visit more enriching.

Seasonal Decor: The Nationality Rooms are often decorated for various holidays and cultural celebrations. You might visit during a time when a room is adorned for a special occasion.

Art and Artifacts: Each room is decorated with authentic art, artifacts, and furnishings that represent the culture it embodies. This attention to detail makes the experience immersive.

Events and Festivals: The Nationality Rooms host cultural events and festivals throughout the year. These events provide an opportunity to experience music, dance, food, and traditions from different cultures.

Before your visit, check the University of Pittsburgh's official website or contact the university for information on visiting hours, guided tours, and any special events or cultural celebrations happening in the Nationality Rooms. Whether you're a cultural enthusiast, a history buff, or someone interested in global diversity, the Nationality Rooms offer a captivating journey into the traditions and architecture of numerous nations and ethnic groups.

108.Attend a performance by PICT Classic Theatre.

Attending a performance by PICT Classic Theatre in Pittsburgh, Pennsylvania, promises an enriching and immersive experience in the world of classic and timeless theatrical productions. Here's what you can expect when you attend a show by PICT Classic Theatre:

PICT Classic Theatre:

Classic and Timeless Works: PICT Classic Theatre is renowned for its commitment to presenting classic plays and works by celebrated playwrights, including William Shakespeare, Anton Chekhov, Oscar Wilde, and many more. You'll have the opportunity to see some of the most enduring and influential plays in the history of theater.

Talented Cast: The company features skilled actors who bring these classic characters and stories to life with depth and authenticity. Their performances often capture the essence of the original productions.

High-Quality Productions: PICT Classic Theatre is known for its dedication to high-quality productions, with attention to period-accurate costumes, sets, and staging, enhancing the authenticity of the experience.

Classic Theater Atmosphere: Attending a performance by PICT Classic Theatre often feels like stepping back in time, with an ambiance that evokes the charm and sophistication of classic theater.

Educational and Cultural Significance: The theater company frequently offers educational programs, lectures, and discussions that provide context and insights into the historical and cultural significance of the classic works they present.

Community Engagement: PICT Classic Theatre engages with the local community and often hosts post-show discussions, Q&A sessions with actors and directors, and special events to encourage audience participation and cultural exchange.

Before attending a performance, check PICT Classic Theatre's official website or local event listings for information on show schedules, ticket availability, and any special events or workshops that may be taking place. Whether you're a theater enthusiast, a lover of classic literature, or someone seeking a refined and culturally rich night out, PICT Classic Theatre offers a captivating journey into the world of classic theater and enduring literary masterpieces.

109.Take a scenic drive through Blue Knob State Park (near Pittsburgh).

Taking a scenic drive through Blue Knob State Park, located in the Allegheny Mountains near Pittsburgh, Pennsylvania, offers a tranquil and picturesque journey through the natural beauty of the region. Here's what you can expect when you embark on a scenic drive around Blue Knob State Park:

Blue Knob State Park:

Mountain Scenery: Blue Knob is known for its stunning mountainous landscapes and dense forests. As you drive through the park, you'll be treated to breathtaking views of the rugged terrain and lush vegetation.

Scenic Byways: The park often features designated scenic byways or roads that take you through the heart of the park's most picturesque areas. These routes are carefully chosen to provide the best views of the landscape.

Picnic Areas: You may find designated picnic areas along the drive, providing opportunities to stop, have a meal, and take in the serene surroundings. These spots are perfect for relaxation and enjoying nature.

Wildlife Observation: Keep an eye out for wildlife such as deer, birds, and various forest creatures. Blue Knob State Park is a haven for nature enthusiasts and birdwatchers.

Hiking and Outdoor Activities: Depending on the season and your interests, you can engage in outdoor activities such as hiking, nature walks, and exploration of the park's trails. The park offers opportunities for a range of recreational activities.

Seasonal Changes: The beauty of Blue Knob varies with the seasons. In spring, you'll see wildflowers in bloom, while autumn brings vibrant foliage. Each season provides a unique and memorable experience.

Before you begin your scenic drive, check Blue Knob State Park's official website or contact the park office for information on road conditions, access points, seasonal activities, and specific park rules and guidelines. Whether you're a nature lover, an outdoor enthusiast, or someone seeking a peaceful escape into the natural beauty of the Pennsylvania mountains, a scenic drive through Blue Knob State Park offers a rejuvenating and captivating journey through the region's pristine landscapes.

110. Visit the Contemporary Craft gallery.

Visiting the Contemporary Craft gallery in Pittsburgh, Pennsylvania, is an opportunity to immerse yourself in the world of contemporary and innovative art and craft. Here's what you can expect when you visit the Contemporary Craft gallery:

Contemporary Craft Gallery:

Cutting-Edge Art and Craft: The gallery showcases cutting-edge works by contemporary artists and craftspersons. You'll encounter a diverse range of artistic expressions that challenge traditional boundaries and explore new materials and techniques.

Rotating Exhibits: The gallery often hosts rotating exhibitions that highlight different artists, themes, and art forms. This means there's always something new and fresh to see on your visit.

Craftsmanship and Creativity: You can explore a wide variety of artistic mediums, including ceramics, textiles, glass, wood, metalwork, and more. The artists often push the boundaries of these mediums, creating unique and thought-provoking pieces.

Educational Opportunities: The Contemporary Craft gallery often offers educational programs, workshops, and artist talks that provide insights into the creative processes and techniques employed by the featured artists.

Art for Sale: Many of the exhibited artworks are available for purchase, making the gallery a great place to discover and collect contemporary art and craft pieces.

Community Engagement: The gallery regularly hosts community events, artist receptions, and art-related activities that encourage interaction with local artists and the art community.

Travel to Pittsburgh Pennsylvania

Before your visit, check the Contemporary Craft gallery's official website or local event listings for information on current exhibitions, hours of operation, admission fees, and any special events or programs that may be taking place. Whether you're an art enthusiast, a collector, or someone interested in the latest trends in contemporary art and craft, the Contemporary Craft gallery offers a dynamic and inspiring journey into the world of contemporary creative expression.

Conclusion

Pittsburgh, Pennsylvania, is a captivating narrative of transformation, resilience, and adaptability. From its early days as a strategic frontier fort, Pittsburgh evolved into a bustling industrial powerhouse during the 19th century. Its growth was propelled by its advantageous geographic location at the confluence of the Monongahela, Allegheny, and Ohio Rivers, which facilitated trade and transportation. The city's abundant natural resources, particularly coal and iron ore, provided the raw materials that fueled its rapid industrialization.

Pittsburgh's prominence as the "Steel City" during the industrial revolution was marked by the production of steel, iron, glass, and other manufactured goods. The city's industrial prowess was a testament to the hard work and ingenuity of its diverse immigrant population. The city's iconic skyline and infrastructure were shaped by this period, with steel mills and factories dominating the landscape.

However, the latter half of the 20th century brought significant challenges as the steel industry faced decline. Economic hardships, environmental pollution, and a shrinking workforce cast a shadow over Pittsburgh. Yet, the city refused to succumb to these challenges and embarked on a remarkable journey of reinvention.

Pittsburgh transformed itself from an industrial giant into a thriving hub of technology, education, healthcare, and culture. The city's embrace of innovation and adaptability led to its rebranding as a center for robotics, medical research, and higher education. The presence of renowned universities, medical institutions, and tech companies highlights Pittsburgh's commitment to progress.

Today, Pittsburgh stands as a testament to the indomitable spirit of its people. The city's diverse neighborhoods celebrate their unique histories and cultures, while its flourishing arts and cultural scene pays homage to its industrial heritage. Pittsburgh's determination to revitalize its riverfronts, redevelop former industrial sites, and foster sustainability initiatives reflects its forward-thinking approach.

In essence, Pittsburgh's history is not merely a relic of the past; it serves as the bedrock for the city's ongoing evolution and growth. The lessons of adaptability, resilience, and the pursuit of innovation from its past continue to guide the city as it shapes its future. Pittsburgh remains a city that embodies the American spirit of progress and reinvention, celebrating its heritage while looking toward the horizon with optimism and ambition.

If you enjoyed, please leave a 5-star Amazon Review

To get a free list of people who knows publishing top places to travel all around the world, click this link
https://bit.ly/peoplewhoknowtravel

References

Rcsprinter123, CC BY-SA 3.0 <https://creativecommons.org/licenses/by-sa/3.0>, via Wikimedia Commons
https://pixabay.com/photos/strawberry-dessert-strawberries-2191973/

Printed in Great Britain
by Amazon